"After reading MaryAnn's *Medium Mentor*, I feel an undeniable connection to my lost loved ones."
— **Maria Menounos**, host of *Better Together with Maria Menounos* and *New York Times* bestselling author of *The EveryGirl's Guide to Life*

"This is the book I needed to read at exactly this moment in time, and I had no idea I needed to read it. As my own intuitive abilities are increasing, and I am ready to shed the skin of people-pleaser and step more into my authentic power and truth, MaryAnn DiMarco provides me with the tools and practices I need to do both. Not only for psychics and mediums, this is a powerful self-help book and guide to bring us closer to our true nature — spiritual beings having a human experience."
— **Kelly Noonan Gores**, writer/director/producer of the *HEAL* documentary

"MaryAnn will help you awaken your inner guide and unlock the power and strength of your intuition. Her work is life-changing!"
— **Marie Forleo**, #1 *New York Times* bestselling author of *Everything Is Figureoutable*

"This book is a true gem — and one I wish I'd had when starting out on my spiritual journey! Acting as a mentor and guide, MaryAnn DiMarco unpacks it all in her refreshingly honest, down-to-earth, and conversational style, helping us navigate the path to unlocking our psychic gifts and intuitive guidance."
— **Rebecca Rosen**, spiritual medium and author of *Spirited*

"MaryAnn is the most gifted psychic and intuitive I know, and she has played a huge role in my own psychic awakening journey. She has been a mentor and guide for many of the biggest milestones in my life and always shares the most loving, profound, and accurate guidance. One of the best things about MaryAnn is that she is both down-to-earth and deeply tuned in to realms beyond, so her wisdom and guidance resonate far and wide. There is a reason I call her my spiritual mama! This book is full of powerful techniques that will no doubt change your life and tune you back in to your heart and soul. If you are looking to expand your mind and spirit, and most of all to connect to realms beyond (and ancestors and loved ones! It's so fun!), this book is for you. I can't wait for you to learn from MaryAnn as I have been so blessed to!"

— **Jordan Younger**, author of *Breaking Vegan*, podcast host, and founder of The Balanced Blonde

"Allow the words on these pages to crack you open to your greatest source of power, inner wisdom, and intuitive guidance. Take a deep breath, and know that you're no longer alone on this journey. You now have your own Medium Mentor."

— from the foreword by **Gabrielle Bernstein**, #1 *New York Times* bestselling author of *The Universe Has Your Back*

MEDIUM MENTOR

MEDIUM MENTOR

10 Powerful Techniques
to Awaken Divine Guidance
for Yourself and Others

MaryAnn DiMarco

with Chandika

Foreword by Gabrielle Bernstein

New World Library
Novato, California

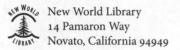 New World Library
14 Pamaron Way
Novato, California 94949

Text design by Tona Pearce Myers

Library of Congress Cataloging-in-Publication Data

Names: DiMarco, MaryAnn, author. | Bernstein, Gabrielle, author of foreword.
Title: Medium mentor : 10 powerful techniques to awaken divine guidance
    for yourself and others / MaryAnn DiMarco with Chandika ; foreword by
    Gabrielle Bernstein.
Description: Novato, California : New World Library, 2022. | Summary: "A
    guidebook that shows ordinary people how to develop clairvoyant or
    psychic abilities via ten proven techniques"-- Provided by publisher.
Identifiers: LCCN 2021057618 (print) | LCCN 2021057619 (ebook) | ISBN
    9781608687633 (paperback) | ISBN 9781608687640 (epub)
Subjects: LCSH: Clairvoyance. | Psychic ability.
Classification: LCC BF1325 .D55 2022 (print) | LCC BF1325 (ebook) |
    DDC 133.8/4--dc23/eng/20220103
LC record available at https://lccn.loc.gov/2021057618
LC ebook record available at https://lccn.loc.gov/2021057619

First printing, April 2022
ISBN 978-1-60868-763-3
Ebook ISBN 978-1-60868-764-0
Printed in Canada on 100% postconsumer-waste recycled paper

 New World Library is proud to be a Gold Certified Environmentally Responsible Publisher. Publisher certification awarded by Green Press Initiative.

10   9   8   7   6   5   4   3   2

For my sweet Mr. Hall. I will forever be your Mrs. Hall. Lifetime after lifetime, always, all ways.

For my amazing children. May you always hear and follow the beautiful guidance of your angels.

And for you, the reader, who inspired me to write this book. May it awaken you to the power of your own abilities so that you can use them in your own life and share them with others.

···)·)•(•(···

CONTENTS

FOREWORD

"Gab, I booked you an awesome segment on *Dr. Oz*! It's all about channeling angels! You'll be on with a medium named MaryAnn DiMarco," my publicist excitedly shared.

"OMG, you know I love a great medium," I replied.

The following week I showed up to the *Dr. Oz* studios several hours early for hair and makeup. I sat down in the makeup chair next to a beautiful woman. Her energy made me feel an instant sense of ease. She smiled at me and said, "I'm MaryAnn. We're on the show together today."

It was love at first sight.

We had an instant connection, and we both intuitively knew that this was not a chance encounter. We knew we'd been guided to meet.

Following the fun segment, MaryAnn met me in my green-room to say goodbye. Then, out of nowhere, she started channeling my guides! Every word out of her mouth was incredibly accurate. She knew things I hadn't shared with anyone. I was blown away by her brilliant ability to listen to Spirit and deliver such clear guidance.

Sure, it was awesome to get an impromptu reading in the greenroom. But what excited me most was that I sensed I could learn from her. I'd been channeling on my own for years, but I didn't trust my own mediumship and therefore kept it to myself. MaryAnn's loving presence and expertise gave me the confidence to ask her for help.

"Can you be my Medium Mentor?" I said.

And the rest is history!

For the past five years MaryAnn has been one of my dearest friends and teachers. Her profound ability to effortlessly channel Spirit has been a source of inspiration for me as I have developed my own connection. Her respect for the art of mediumship has given me clear boundaries on how to connect to the spiritual realm. And her decades of experience have been infused into all our mentoring sessions. Each time MaryAnn offers me a personal reading, she teaches me something new about my own ability to connect to Spirit.

I know deep in my heart that MaryAnn was placed in my life to help me confidently commit to my mediumship. This is her greatest gift: her desire to serve other spiritual people who want to connect to, translate, and access spiritual guidance for the highest good for all. Each student she works with expands their own inner ability to listen to the divine wisdom of Spirit and carry the messages in their own communities. Her ability to teach and guide has helped thousands of people around the globe. When one channel awakens, a new light shines upon the world.

If you've opened this book, it means you're ready to contribute to that light. You're ready to ground yourself in your own ability to channel and claim your mediumship.

Allow the words on these pages to crack you open to your greatest source of power, inner wisdom, and intuitive guidance. Take a deep breath, and know that you're no longer alone on this journey. You now have your own Medium Mentor.

— **Gabrielle Bernstein**, #1 *New York Times* bestselling author of *The Universe Has Your Back*

PREFACE

A few years ago, I found myself in a large, crowded room. It felt like every pair of eyes — probably two hundred of them — was fixed on me. The facial expressions varied. Some were nervous, while others were smiling or sad. Most, however, were eager. The people assembled wanted *something*. Perhaps relief from their suffering after the loss of a loved one. Maybe an affirmation that psychic mediums are real. It could even be entertainment. Their degree of belief or skepticism varied, but they were all listening, regardless. To anyone using their ears alone, the room was silent. The attentive faces watched me move through the crowd, waiting, hoping I would choose them to receive a message from Spirit.

Little did they know, I was waiting, too. The truth is that I don't choose anyone; Spirit does. I had been approached by the organizers of this fundraiser to offer something interesting to their attendees — something that would ensure they would show up, have a good time, and contribute to the cause. And by that point in my career as a psychic medium, I was confident I would be able to deliver. Spirit speaks to me anytime I ask, especially in a situation with so many people around, so much to say. But I never know what's going to happen. I may or may not even fully remember what I say aloud. I just ground myself and let the light come through.

The event's attendees were not speaking. Yet from my vantage point, the room was *loud*. Spirit was vying for my attention. Like spiritual hecklers, numerous voices yelled seemingly random words into my inner ear to pull me toward their friends or family; they all just wanted to be heard. My role was to sort through them and find the clearest message. I remained calm and in charge as I asked my guides to help me focus the many voices, quiet my own thoughts, and allow the words from the Other Side to come through in a more orderly fashion.

As I did so, a single word began to take shape. At first, it felt and sounded like a thought, but as it formed, I realized it had a different quality somehow — one that was familiar, known to me. It was detached from my own thoughts but still felt as if it were coming through me. And it was unmistakable. As I tuned in to it, the word became louder. *PIZZA*.

I let my mind alight on the word, and suddenly, all my senses focused on the idea of pizza. There was none in the room — in fact, there was no food at the event at all — but I smelled pizza, tasted pizza, felt its texture in my mouth, saw a full pie in my mind's eye. I knew it was Spirit communicating with me. This particular spirit, in his quest to pull my focus away from the other voices, engaged all five senses, a tricky move that was immediately effective; within seconds, pizza was all I was able to think about, all I could imagine. I was flooded with memories of eating pizza. I was dreaming up my favorite toppings.

I allowed myself to be fully immersed in the experience of pizza, just waiting. Then I felt it: the psychic pull. The message about pizza was for someone behind me. I followed my urge, turned around, and walked toward a table across the room without hesitation.

It took me a minute to get there, and the people at the table began to shift uncomfortably as they realized they had been chosen. The others around just watched. As I approached, the energy within me began to build into an excited, higher vibration. The spirit continued to speak as I walked, identifying himself and offering further details while still repeating *pizza, pizza, pizza,* a chaotic buzz coming to a crescendo. Despite the rising energy, I felt calm; I trusted Spirit completely, knowing my guides were at work and my boundaries were in place, and I observed as everything came together in a perfectly orchestrated series of occurrences happening at lightning speed. I cataloged all the information, trying to organize it into words, and from there into sentences. I looked at the ten or so people at the table, none of whom I had ever met, and tapped into the deep sadness that accompanies loss. I could feel their grief acutely, yet I smiled, because I knew Spirit was about to ease their pain. I looked each of them in the eye and opened my mouth.

"There is a man named Joseph with me. He is yelling the word *pizza* at me and telling me to come talk to you. You guys must really love pizza!"

The woman directly across from me was the first to speak, tears in her eyes. She said, "My dad Joseph just passed. We are a family who owns pizza restaurants."

It was time for Joseph and me to get to work.

Everyone Needs a Mentor

I have been receiving messages like this all my life, but it wasn't until I started consciously developing myself as a psychic medium that I could make any sense of them. I have always known that I was somewhat psychic. I suspect that you, too, have a nagging sense that you have an above-average intuitive gift. Like Joseph's refrain, *pizza*, that nagging voice has become louder and louder, pulling you toward these words.

Everyone needs mentorship when they're developing a skill. I certainly did. Before I started working with my gifts, I often mistook channeled messages for my own strong opinions. I was born on Long Island with strong Italian roots, and I'm not afraid to be opinionated — or to be loud about it. Perhaps if someone like Joseph had come to me thirty years ago, I would have just left the event and gotten a slice of pizza, even if I wasn't really hungry. It took a lot of study to realize that many of my opinions weren't mine at all — they were channeled. As I've worked on myself, finding the tools and tricks that are most effective for me, I've learned to separate what's mine from what's not. I've learned how to deliver messages, and when, and to whom. I've learned which messages are only for me and which ones are meant to be shared. And now, I've learned how to walk other psychic mediums through the process.

I came into my role as a psychic medium slowly but willingly. I wrote about my background in greater detail in my first book, *Believe, Ask, Act: Divine Steps to Raise Your Intuition, Create Change, and Discover Happiness*, so I'll just provide a quick summary here. My childhood was typical in many ways and decidedly atypical in others. Like many in the 1970s, my mother became interested in meditation. She first taught me to sit quietly and work to silence my thoughts when I was just five years old. From there, she started working with her own psychic gifts, which opened her to see my latent abilities. I had a sense when I was a child that I could be psychic, but I didn't do much with it. When I was a teenager, my mother went to see a young medium on Long Island who had gained local, but certainly not widespread, fame: John Edward. Today, John is quite famous for his skill set, but at the time he was still operating out of his home. He told my mother that she had a highly psychic daughter with mediumistic talent and firmly stated that I would need to work to develop my gifts.

I believed John, as did my mother. In fact, I believed all of it: that Spirit speaks to those willing to listen, and that some of us are particularly adept at communicating with those who have passed and sharing their messages, while others are merely meant to communicate with their own guides to help them move through life with increased ease. I had a sense of which category I was in. I furthered my interest with practices here and there as a young adult. Yet I wasn't fully ready to do the work. I wanted to live a "normal" life first.

So I did. I went to college and got a job. I got married and had two amazing kids. I loved and lost several people close to me. And in that process, I continued to dabble in mediumship; I heard Spirit speak from time to time, let intuition guide my decisions frequently, and allowed hazy visions of the future into my mind. But it wasn't until my midthirties that several smaller life crises, including my divorce and grief from deep losses, convened into one big sense of suffering. Suddenly, I knew it was time.

That's where this book comes in. It's part of *your* time. You are being called by something greater than you can ever imagine. And I want to be clear that I am not the one answering that call, nor do I have all the answers; you are, and your guides do. I'm just here to facilitate that process, as my mentor facilitated it for me.

In the early 2000s, in the midst of my internal crisis, I dialed the number of an intuitive who had been recommended to me. Or, at least, I *thought* she had been recommended to me — I later found out that the person who had been doing the recommending actually pointed me toward someone else. The divine intervened, and I found myself on the phone with Pat Longo, a healer and teacher who lived about an hour away from me. Pat invited me to one of her classes, and a few days later, I drove out to her home to attend my first course in developing intuitive ability. I ended up attending these classes for years, faithfully making the hour-plus journey each way, and they opened me to my gift as a psychic medium. They represented the first step in bringing me to where I am today. I am forever grateful for Pat's tutelage. If your path includes channeling messages for others, and perhaps even making a profession out of it, similar classes with a trusted intuitive will be a necessary step for you to take at some point.

That said, some guidance is universal, so I've gathered some of the most valuable tips I offer my students here. I wrote this book to present a broad and adaptable framework for your individual process as you consciously develop your intuition. It's meant to help you connect with Spirit freely throughout your day-to-day life, whenever you need support and assistance, while also giving context to the things that are likely happening to and around you as a sensitive being. I've included examples from my friends, students, and clients, changing all their names to protect their privacy, as well as anecdotes from my own life. It's my sincere hope that by the time you reach the final page, you'll be in a working dialogue with Spirit. You'll have a personal, unique connection to the psychic plane, and you'll be able to channel your own prayers, use your own imagination, and access your own wisdom throughout the process.

Developing your intuition will not make your life perfect. It isn't like having a Magic 8 Ball to tell you what move to make at a given point of time. It won't necessarily tell you when to quit your job, whether you should move, or where you left your car keys. Sometimes, these things come through as a fringe benefit, but they aren't the point. Instead, it will help you trust your own decision-making, because you'll come to realize you're never making any of those decisions alone. If you were born with these gifts, on some level you're always listening to *someone*. Turning your innate abilities into honed skills will help you be sure you're attuned to the frequencies of the highest light, which in turn will give you the confidence you need to move forward with grace.

That confidence ripples outward. If you're a people pleaser, watch out; doing this work is going to force you to start living your truth, becoming your full, no-holds-barred, authentic self. The easy answer for why this happens is that psychics are forced to learn to set boundaries with Spirit, and doing so makes them a lot better at setting boundaries with people. This doesn't need to be offensive or aggressive, and in the long term it will certainly be a more comfortable way to live, but in the short term this transformation may be slightly uncomfortable. Don't worry; your guides will be with you every step of the way. It's their job to help you find your own right path.

Why Now?

My guides suggested I write a book — and then they insisted that I do so *right now*. There's a reason for that. You, too, may have noticed that your guides are more communicative lately. It seems like collectively, spirit guides are waking people up left and right, calling people to their higher purpose, whatever that may be. Thank goodness for that! These are tense times. We're confronting many uncertainties, and not only do we not know what's happening next, but it's feeling increasingly unlikely things will go on as they did before. Social hierarchies are being questioned and overturned; our way of working, and working with each other, has shifted drastically; even the planet itself is changing, and rapidly. In the midst of all this, much is in the realm of mystery. Yet our own intuition doesn't have to be difficult to access. Each of us has the power to connect intuitively, and once we activate that power, the response that is right for us becomes clear.

In *Believe, Ask, Act*, I devoted a lot of attention to getting through life's roadblocks using a simple, three-step method. The basics of that method — believing, asking for guidance, and acting on the guidance we receive — are woven throughout these pages as well. With this book I take it a step further, encouraging you to connect with your guidance for a wider range of reasons. We don't have to wait for roadblocks; our guides are there for us anytime we need them!

I've been called to demystify this process so that as we face these massive shifts, we're prepared. As a global community, we're being called to spiritually awaken; strengthening our communication with the Other Side can only help us do so. Everyone has an innate knowing lying dormant within them — a forgotten ability just waiting to be recalled. Developing that can help you prepare for the next thing to come along, whether that's a shift in social consciousness; a move in your own life, such as a new relationship or job or home; or even a major unforeseen event, like a global pandemic.

When you're comfortable accessing your intuition, you never have to think about what to do in a curveball circumstance like that. Just tap in ("Um ... guides? Loved ones? Hello? What do I do now?") and wait for the answer. I'm serious! If the answer doesn't come, it wasn't time yet, plain and simple. And you can access your intuitive guidance anywhere, anytime.

Sure, it helps to set the stage a bit — get out a crystal, maybe, or a deck of oracle cards — but when you're already engaged in an ongoing conversation, you actually don't need any tools. In the most critical moments, you probably won't even have time for that. Doing this work ensures that when you need help, asking for it will be an automatic response.

It's become an automatic response for me, at least, and I've observed a similar shift in many of my students. It's my hope that the same will be true for you.

HOW TO KNOW YOU'RE PSYCHIC

Developing a Common Understanding

S o how do you know you're psychic?
Well, that starts with realizing that on some level, everybody is.

There's an awful lot of mystery surrounding psychic energy in modern culture. On one hand, we're comfortable with understanding that intuition plays a large role in our daily lives ("I had a gut feeling I should buy that house!" or "Yikes — that person gave me the creeps, even before they opened their mouth"). We're rather drawn toward spontaneity, excited by people who seem comfortable living in the moment and allowing positive experiences to come their way. On the other hand, we tend to look down on those who rely on their intuition *too* much to effectively fit into society. If someone's spontaneity turns into chaotic disorganization, we're generally less attracted to it, and when so-called intuitive guidance turns into last-minute, knee-jerk decision-making, it often brings more judgment than admiration.

I'd like to gently suggest that perhaps *being psychic* isn't the issue here — it's what we do with it. Understanding that is a major step toward demystifying the psychic experience. It allows us to lean into the psychic energy flow that serves us and away from the fear-based thoughts that don't. From this perspective, it's easy to see that everyone is psychic — it's just that the bona fide professional psychics have developed a skill set around that discernment.

If that's the case, doesn't it make sense for every one of us to invest in our psychic development? This investment mostly comprises time, attention, and repetition. And whether you intend to read for others or are looking for more guidance only for yourself, dedicating yourself to the pursuit of deeper intuition will *always* achieve results.

In fact, it's precisely what your Team has been leading you to do all along.

Your New Best Friends

In the last few pages, I've referenced terms like *Spirit, Team, guides, gifts,* and *psychic medium.* Let's take a moment to get clear on what these terms mean and how I will be using them throughout this book, as well as to go over the basic precepts that form the foundation of my work.

Spirit is the collective name for universal energy, including all beings on the Other Side. Sometimes I use it as a synonym for God, but I'm more likely to use *Source, universe,* or even *the light* to get at that same idea, which for me all speak to the same benevolent, universal energy that connects and guides us. Each one of us is blessed to be supported by our own *Universal Team* made up of guides, loved ones, and angels. We tap into their guidance through our intuition. We are all born with intuition; everyone is, therefore, naturally intuitive. We are also all capable of empathy, or *feeling* others, which often takes the form of mirroring the thoughts and emotions of the people around us. These are human traits. They exist in the human realm. Imagine a radio tuned to the lowest frequency. Many people suffer for being empaths, especially when they take on the low-vibration energy of others. Carrying our own heavy energy is enough; carrying other people's is just exhausting! I feel that the word *empath* is quite overused in this context. As I see it, the issue isn't an abundance of empathy — it's a lack of boundaries.

We also are all somewhat psychic, which means we can tap into a higher vibration and pick up on the energy around us that way. This is one way to dispel some of that dense energy. *Frequency* is trained vibration. This means with proper instruction and enough practice, some of us can learn to choose, elevate, and sustain our vibration, intentionally aligning ourselves with a certain frequency. It's like tuning the radio of our perception up a few megahertz so we can hear what's happening on a different station. Sometimes this means we can even predict things that haven't happened yet or see things that are not connected to us in the physical realm at all, like something that happened across the globe. That can happen by accident or, when a person chooses to work with their psychic ability, intentionally. That means a trained psychic can say, "I don't know exactly what's happening on the human level, but I'm going to raise my vibration so I can understand it on a psychic level," and then they can shift to another frequency and listen in. That's how psychics tap into other people's energy and read them. So while those who easily perceive the thoughts or feelings of living people are empaths (and yes, most psychics are naturally empathic), when we can really tap into someone else's *energy* and read them from a higher-vibrational standpoint, we're exercising our *psychic gifts*.

By consciously developing our psychic ability, some of us begin to develop our mediumistic ability as well. That's because the more we practice tuning the radio, finding the exact station we want, and then maintaining the connection, the better we get at this process. For some of us, this means shifting to the highest frequencies, which is where mediumship can take place. A *medium* is a person who can connect and communicate directly with Spirit. (Since all mediums are also psychic, many call themselves *psychic mediums*.) The easy way to explain this is to say that mediums speak to those on the Other Side. Mediums can often receive specific information about the loved ones they are communicating with, perceiving their personalities and opinions. They can receive messages and deliver them to a *sitter*, someone who requests a reading from a psychic or psychic medium. For me, that's fairly easy, but that isn't everyone's path.

If that feels disappointing, I have good news. Our guides and loved ones can reach us on nearly any frequency. Some of the practices in this book are aimed at helping you shift your vibration and start sustaining it, while others will help you call your Team to come talk to you where you are. Guides have plenty of methods, from shifting their own frequency to sending you messages through the other people in your life. When you know how to ask, you can put in a request for communication, a sign, or a dream, and they are usually happy to comply. My role is to teach you how to do just that!

I often refer to people who choose to develop their psychic gifts, dedicating them to the greater good of all concerned, as *spiritual Lightworkers*. Spiritual lightwork includes devising a unique, personal methodology that we can use to connect with our Universal Team, creating a back-and-forth dialogue. Our Team is always looking out for us; we can call on them to sweep through a room of people, cleaning up low-vibration energies, or to protect us when things get tough. Powerful, right? Wherever we are in the world, our guides are there to direct us — as long as we're willing to listen.

That "listening" can take many forms. Because we are in human bodies that perceive the physical world through our five senses, the spiritual world uses this same method to get through to us. Our senses — sight, smell, hearing, taste, and touch — are the portals through which Spirit communicates. (More on that in chapter 3.) And because we, as humans, also possess memory and creativity, Spirit often uses our existing frame of reference to get through as well. That means that our own imagination and personality are Spirit's primary ways to guide us forward. (I have a lot more to say about that in chapter 4.)

Everyone possesses these abilities, but few develop them without instruction or mentorship. We live in a world where it's rare for anyone to be taught how to do this. That's why I'm dedicated to walking you through the process. In fact, most of us were taught *not* to develop our abilities as children. We were taught to fear our own connection with the Other Side. And the tragedy there is that this very fear has made it more difficult to access our greatest source of guidance.

Once you've tuned in to it, it will always be up to you to put the guidance into action using free will. Your Team is your posse, the best set of friends you never knew you had, and once you get to know your peeps, you'll realize you're never alone — ever. They'll always guide you, but they can't *force* you to do anything. Each one of us is accountable for acting on the guidance we receive. That starts with trusting that it's real.

You're Not Crazy, Just Connected

If I could name the single word that is most often repeated when I read for people or work with students — you know, one that isn't *Spirit* or *medium* or *and* or *the* — it's *crazy*.

"I always thought I was a little crazy..." a student might confess, just after perfectly delivering a message from another student's loved one. Or a client might whisper, "That's just crazy..." as I recount details from his childhood I have no earthly way of knowing. And then there's my favorite: "This might sound crazy, but..." To me, nearly every time, the information that comes after that "but" isn't crazy at all. In fact, this is usually what someone says right before they drop the psychic's informational equivalent of solid gold.

When people refer to "crazy" in the context of psychic development, they're not referring to diagnosable mental illness. They're referring to a degree of wooey that is socially inappropriate; they're referring to a fear that possessing or developing psychic gifts is going to make it harder, perhaps even impossible, to interact with the people and environments around them. Here, *crazy* means "weird," "bizarre," "unacceptable," "disruptive," "absurd," and above all, "foolish."

I'm living proof that despite their fears, that does not have to be their destiny. I often answer with the refrain: "If you're crazy, I'm certifiable." And it's true. I've dedicated my life to retrieving information from one energetic plane and delivering it to another. I've placed myself on the bridge between worlds and chosen to live there. And instead of being, you know, *subtle* about it, I've gone ahead and made my position in this wild mess fully public.

Yet in basically all other ways, I'm as normal as can be. I live in a home I love and have a fantastic family. My friends are lovely and supportive. I'm routinely told that I "don't look like a psychic" — whatever that means! I grocery shop and go to the gym, just like everybody else; yeah, I balance my chakras and talk to the dead, but I'm just not that weird about it. At least, I don't make it any weirder than it has to be.

Let's establish a few things. First, having an intuitive gift does not make you crazy. It is not weird to sense, feel, or communicate things you do not initially understand — people have been doing this since time immemorial. Second, if you count these experiences as some of the most profound in your life, you're certainly not alone. In fact, you're in good company. Many perfectly lovely people have these experiences. And third, using your conscious will to develop your innate talent on the path of a spiritual Lightworker is hardly the thing that's going to push you over the edge. On the contrary, it may be one of the sanest things you will ever do.

This Stuff Happens All the Time!

As we normalize psychic knowing, we increase our capacity to recognize psychic events. A sudden psychic event often feels quite unusual in the life of the person experiencing it. Those types of spot-on, could-not-possibly-be-just-coincidence events, wherein information is passed from one realm to another or something is confirmed beyond a shadow of a doubt, can be shocking. They're memorable. And when we don't know how to classify them, it's common to file them away in a sort of you'll-never-believe-this slot in our minds, whose contents are to be revealed only to those we deem trustworthy, and even then with great caution. Many people have at least one experience that fits into that mental filing cabinet.

I know this because many people share these experiences with me. It makes things like cocktail parties delightfully predictable; there I am, standing by a cheese platter, when someone I barely know launches into telling me about a spontaneous psychic event that was clearly an outlier in her experience of life. When students first come to my classes, they're often excited to share a story with me. Maybe they were wishing they could call Grandma and then, suddenly, the phone rang. Perhaps they were remembering a deceased loved one when they coincidentally noticed a sign from that person. Or a song that reminded them of a loved one got stuck in their head, and then it appeared on the radio. These mysterious-seeming events are exciting, and people talk about them in earnest!

This enthusiasm is understandable, and it makes sense to want to check in with a kind soul who will take it seriously. Early in our psychic awakening, we often rely heavily on external confirmation, because it's somehow still hard to believe that psychic connection is possible.

I've had this experience myself. Even when I trust my gift, it's useful to have it validated. About a year into my official psychic education, I began to perceive that I was being followed around by the spirit of a child. This was the sweetest little soul; he didn't do or say much, but he was just always nearby. He would sit in the back seat of my car, appear next to me on the sofa, and even accompany me to the grocery store. A major, highly publicized disaster had recently taken place, and I had a nagging sense that he was one of the children who died there. Yet it seemed so implausible that one of the victims would talk to *me* that I brushed off the thought as a weird extension of my empathy. "All right, MaryAnn, you're seeing the spirit of a deceased child, and that's OK," I told myself, trying to smooth over how foreign that felt. "But you don't get to connect that to what's on the news."

The boy continued to follow me. Kids are really insistent little energies when they want to get a message to their families. Then an old friend called me out of the blue. We took some time to catch up, and in doing so, she mentioned that her brother-in-law was related to one of the victims of the disaster. Sure enough, it was a young boy. Tentatively, I described the personality and appearance of the boy who had been following me around. She gasped. It was him. Together, we grieved his loss — and shared in the excitement of him making contact through me.

Even after my upbringing (which, as I explained in the preface, was super open to these things), even after a year of dedicated courses in psychic mediumship, even after coming to grips with the fact that I was *definitely* being accompanied by the spirit of a deceased young boy, I still really needed this validation. By now, I've been consciously channeling, and spending time around other psychics, enough to definitively declare that these events are quite common. I don't need as much validation, in part because I understand that the idea that psychics, psychic mediums, and psychic events or spontaneous psychic experiences are rare is a myth.

The more commonplace nature of psychic experiences is further highlighted when we consider the ones many of us never file away as psychic events at all. I'm talking about the sign that says "Garage Sale" and inspires a U-turn, diverting us away from the major car accident that occurs seconds later up ahead. Or the feeling that we're going to meet someone important today, followed by our meeting someone important today. These sorts of events often just get chalked up to luck or good timing. It's only when we're deep in our journey of development as spiritual Lightworkers that we come to recognize them as psychic events, too.

Frequently, psychic events can come to a sort of crescendo at some point in a lifetime. That crescendo often calls people to start developing their psychic gifts, to start really doing the lightwork they came here to do. In other cases, the upswell begins after a particularly gifted person starts working with their psychic mediumship. It's as if they had their thumb in the dam the whole time, and the second they take it out — *pop!* — the waters pour forth.

My student Keri's mediumship opened like that. In one of her very first classes, she delivered a clear, unmistakable message from another student's son who had passed. Over the next couple of months, Keri learned she was a remarkable medium; she received message after message, many of them completely spot-on. I can look at her, even over video conference, and know she has something to deliver — and this has been true since early on in her work with me. At first, this sort of freaked her out! She doesn't really want to talk to the dead; her guides have told her she's a healer. Yet they've also told her to keep doing this work, and now she's realizing it's because to truly heal others, she needs to understand the frequency of mediumship. Keri is developing her psychic gifts so that Spirit can instruct her healing work, and her clients will be none the wiser. At first, she was overwhelmed by her psychic experiences. She needed help and mentorship to sort through it all. In time, she has become much more comfortable with the process. She sets strong boundaries (more on that in chapter 3), which allow her to welcome everything that is happening, and she acknowledges her doubts about psychic mediumship without giving in to them.

Putting Doubt Aside

A major part of this path is learning to put our doubt aside. It can be so hard to trust that what we see, feel, and/or hear is divine guidance! I've been teaching long enough that by this point, I've managed to identify several distinct patterns of doubt in my students as they develop their psychic gifts.

Some students just waltz into the room, unafraid. Their arrival in class cues the opening of the floodgates, and the psychic energy just flows. These rare souls, like Keri, are the envy of their peers because this stuff just comes easily to them. Validating experiences pour in before doubt can even get involved, and by the time it does, these students have plenty of strong memories to lean into. If you are one of these people, embrace that confidence, and if you're not, don't worry.

Other students sort of nervously slink into the room, eyes darting from face to face to evaluate whether it's emotionally safe to be there. These folks are often slow to deliver a message, even when what they're receiving feels crystal clear to me. They often second-guess themselves and end their sentences with unintentional question marks, regardless of how immediately and specifically they can answer their own questions. For instance, during one workshop, my student Jess saw a pair of hands, fingers pointed upward, holding an apple. That's a pretty clear image, isn't it? But for Jess, it wasn't. Jess's voice was high and tight as she said, "I ... well, I saw, um, some hands? Like this?" She tentatively demonstrated the hand position. "And holding, like, I think, maybe, a red apple?" From there, we began to discuss possible interpretations: an apple could mean a teacher, a farm, health, or any number of things to Jess. The one thing I knew for sure was that Jess *did* receive a message.

Most students are somewhere on the spectrum between these two extremes, often bouncing off either end temporarily.

They have moments of triumph and total confidence followed by moments when doubt threatens to consume them completely. The idea of being not good enough is inherently ego based, and it arises in so many ways! A student may show up with confidence before flipping over to doubt, or the exact opposite, sometimes within just a few minutes.

A display of evidential mediumship — with its immediate power to stop people in their tracks, causing them to no longer wonder *if* but *how* — seems like the most surefire way to blast through this doubt. This is the experience of successfully delivering a piece of evidence, especially when it is well received, and providing external confirmation such that even the most skeptical people are shocked. Yet it takes time and sustained effort to nurture a gift like that. It took *me* time, at least. This is part of why, outside the supportive environment of a classroom or a trade session with a friend, I don't recommend you read anyone based solely on the information contained within the pages of this book.

It's difficult to slay doubt completely; for most of us, this process takes time. And during that time, we're often quite sensitive. Our doubt can be influenced, for better or worse, by others. And in our enthusiasm, we can cross others' boundaries — that's right, the boundaries of the living.

If we become overly excited by our psychic experiences and share them with people whose doubt is strong — especially early in our development as spiritual Lightworkers, when we are learning to understand and properly interpret the messages we receive — we're unlikely to receive the encouragement we want. In many ways, it's also the encouragement we *need*, and it's definitely the encouragement we *deserve*. We may even receive active *dis*couragement, which is entirely unhelpful to our doubt-slaying venture.

There's another issue at play here: if we share our gift with people who don't willingly consent to receiving it, it's not exactly spiritual lightwork. I receive messages all the time that I don't deliver simply because they haven't been solicited. This is a basic consent issue, and it rests on the idea of accountability.

I'll address accountability throughout these pages, but for now, what you need to know is that each one of us is accountable for the energy we share with others. We are accountable for what we call toward us, what we nurture, and what we emanate. When we align ourselves with love and light, it's no problem. Our actions tend to be socially appropriate; we share when we know it will be well received, which is in the very best interest of the recipient. That's part of what makes it lightwork. By doing this, we know our actions are in lockstep with our intention. This significantly reduces the amount of judgment we receive — both behind our backs and to our faces — and when we *are* judged, it's easier to not worry about it. What others think of us is not our business; we're not accountable for that, nor should we be. Our alignment is what matters.

If that's the case, then how do we routinely realign ourselves with love and light? How do we best position ourselves to increase our trust in the guidance we receive? It's an ongoing practice, one that I'll be addressing throughout this book — but a pair of simple rituals can help.

Your Spiritual Home Base

To help us stay connected to the positive, I recommend a pair of foundational practices to *cleanse* and *ground*. Many cultures have a ritualistic cleansing practice, often done with smoke or water, to help remove negative or stagnant energy. There are also numerous practices that point to the idea of grounding: connecting oneself to the body and the earth while calling upon divine energy for support. These rituals involve regularly removing what does not serve us and recommitting our entire being — and, specifically, our body — to the pure channeling of love and light.

Without these practices, things don't flow the way they should. This creates a breeding ground for doubt. At best, we feel discomfort, which makes it hard to keep doing the work we need to do. At worst, stagnant energy hangs around us. We feel like we're losing touch with reality; our doubt goes off the charts. This is an unfortunate state to be in and entirely unnecessary, at that. We're better off if we prevent it altogether.

Choose a way to clean your space, your body, and any sacred objects you hold dear. I encourage this level of freedom, this DIY-style spirituality, with everything. That means if you want to cleanse with incense, go for it. If you want to burn sage or palo santo or some other raw plant, that's fantastic. If you're into holy water, or tap water with essential oils, or even water you've collected from your favorite forest stream, dot a little on your heart or your third eye (the seat of your intuition, located on your forehead between your brows), or perhaps pour a bit on your head or hands. You can say a prayer while you do so, sing a song, recite a mantra, or empty your mind of all thoughts. Pay special attention to the parts of your physical or spiritual body that feel energetically significant — your heart, your hands, your third eye, and so on. What matters most is that you're putting intention toward releasing what doesn't serve.

The same principle applies to grounding. Grounding is about protection. It's about staying present enough to guard our own house, and to ask our guides to join us in that. In most cases, we physically get low to the ground — think praying, sitting in meditation, and so forth — or at least bring attention to the lower parts of the body. Then we ask for help from something outside us. By reconnecting with the light, we remind ourselves of what our spirit is here to do — inhabit this body, for a time, and use that time wisely. We then allow divine energy to come through us, filling us up with positivity and replenishing our resources.

As with cleansing, there are many ways to go about grounding. If you feel connected to a cultural tradition that makes that happen, practice that. If you're called to make up your own thing or to adapt a version of someone else's teaching, that's fine, too. How you protect yourself is your business; my only goal is to convince you to do so.

When I use words like *cleanse, ground*, and *protect*, I don't want to give the impression that there's something dirty or unsafe about spiritual lightwork, because I don't believe that to be the case. Instead, we owe these rituals to ourselves and our Team as a sign of respect. We don't allow anything to build up, any outside energies to cling to us. We hold ourselves accountable by affirming, over and over again, what we're here to do: to work with light while in a human body. Repeating these practices over and over is a necessary part of turning toward a spiritual life.

In summary: find your thing, pick your way, and do it regularly. I'm a stickler about that last part. The more you work on your psychic development, the more you can do these practices — at least once a week is good, and every day is even better. As you practice cleansing and grounding, you will start to know when you need them. These rituals will become comforting; they will become your spiritual home base.

PRACTICE

·· ·)) ᴏ ((·· ·

Smudging and Bringing In the Light

You may have already identified the cleansing and grounding practices that are going to work best for you. If you are still curious, I offer my own. My cleansing practice is *smudging* with sage, and my grounding practice is an adapted visualization meditation that I call *Bringing In the Light*.

Smudging

We'll start with smudging. This is a technique developed in numerous Native American traditions that uses smoke to cleanse the air, which in turn can clear any energetic nastiness hanging on to people, animals, places, and the like. While the act largely mirrors similar incense- and smoke-cleansing methods from Europe, East Asia, and the Middle East, using white sage — my preferred plant for cleansing — is unique to the indigenous communities from the North American continent. White sage has a powerful and immediate effect.

To smudge, light the tip of a single dried leaf or the end of a smudge stick, putting your intention into the flame before blowing it out and allowing the plant to smolder. I love the smell; it immediately opens me up to Spirit. Then, using a small bowl or other sacred item (I like using an abalone shell) to catch any burning pieces that might fall, wave a feather to direct the smoke around your space, clearing out everything that isn't for your own highest good and that of others. Move the smoke over your whole body, being sure to cleanse your hands, heart, and third eye. When you're finished, you can allow the sage to burn out on its own in the bowl, or if it's very well lit, consider putting it out in a little bit of sand or fresh soil.

Bringing In the Light

Bringing In the Light is a mini-meditation based on one I learned from my teacher Pat Longo. This grounding ritual helps us replenish our energy directly from the source. It offers us a protective energy boost while spreading universal Source energy throughout the world. This practice is done seated with the palms facing up.

Start by saying, either internally or aloud, "Dear guides, with gratitude I ask that you fill my body and soul with your love and protection. Please ground my energy so that I may serve the greater good with a renewed vibration." Feel your body connected to the earth. See your own energy reaching down to the planet's very core. Then imagine a bright beam of light coming from above and filling you with divine energy. If visualization comes easily to you, it's possible that you will actually see this light in your mind's eye. If you've never in your life been able to "see" things in your mind's eye, don't worry — just imagine it. Allow the light to enter in through the top of your head, beaming down through your face, and allow some of it to expand outward through your ears, sending forth all the knowledge of the universe. Allow the light to continue descending through your throat, neck, chest, and shoulders; into your arms; and through your fingertips. Allow it to move down through your torso and belly and down your legs to come out your feet. See the light connecting you directly to the floor (if you're indoors) and the earth beneath it. Now, allow that light to ground you even further. Take a few breaths, feeling how the light grounds you. When you're ready, open your eyes.

I encourage you to adapt this ritual for your own needs over time. You will likely learn to do it quickly, sometimes even imperceptibly, as needed. The more you do so, the more you'll be able to recognize when your energy requires a slight adjustment to realign with Spirit.

Getting to Work

In the next chapters, I'll present ten powerful techniques to help further, or jump-start, your connection to the divine guidance that is available to you. These aren't unique to me — many teachers touch on similar topics, and each one of us interprets them slightly differently.

First, we'll look at ego, which is (and should be) an ongoing process for every psychic, regardless of where they are in their development. In chapter 2 we'll move on to fear, which is another topic most psychics return to again and again. In chapter 3 we'll address clairs — our psychic senses — and boundaries, two seemingly unconnected topics that are both essential to understanding our unique psychic structure. Chapter 4 continues the discussion by explaining how each one of us can step into our role as active interpreters of the psychic messages we receive. Chapter 5 gives an overview of the spiritual tools that can help us on our way. In chapter 6 we'll consider how we can best deliver messages with care, concern, and compassion. Chapter 7 helps us cement everything we learned into a sustained spiritual practice. Chapter 8 takes this deeper, looking at how to balance spirituality with the rest of our lives. Then chapter 9 explores how we can put everything we have learned into action through service. Finally, in chapter 10, we'll discuss how to walk the path of light going forward — the ultimate test of positivity and self-worth.

You may have noticed that I focus on the DIY aspect of psychic development, and you'll get more of that in the chapters that follow. I always encourage you to do what you want with the techniques offered in this book, using them as often or as little as you like and absolutely adapting them however you feel guided to adapt them. This can be spontaneous ("going rogue" in the middle of a guided meditation) or long-term (reciting a specific prayer before starting a practice, every time). I may not necessarily know what's best for you, but I can certainly help you access the part of you that does. Together, these ten techniques offer you much of what you need to build a healthy and productive relationship with your guides, regardless of whether you're just looking for more connection in your daily life or you intend to read, coach, or heal professionally. They represent the culmination of everything I have learned in my career as a psychic medium and a mentor to Lightworkers. I have gathered and presented them here so that you can receive the divine wisdom that is intended for *you*.

Chapter One

CHECK YOUR EGO

Discovering Authentic Self-Worth

The first technique to help channel the universe's energy is to get the ego in check. That means we need to take a good hard look at our desire to get overly involved in what we channel, gently moving ourselves out of the way while holding an intention for the highest good for all concerned.

This is a lifelong process. Ego is tricky. It rears up when we least expect it, sometimes in an obvious way. Other times, it's sneaky and underhanded, guiding our movements from the shadows. We are accountable for knowing our own ego well and noticing when it's activated. It's our job to keep our ego from disrupting the spiritual lightwork we came here to do.

In this chapter, we'll look at what ego is and how it works. We'll consider how to know when it's activated within us, as well as understand how that might look to an outside observer. I'll outline my three top ways to work with the ego. Then you'll try out a chakra meditation to see where the ego is most active at this point in time. When you put all the pieces together, you'll be left with a strong understanding of how to continue the ongoing work of ego management, which is essential to keeping you and your gifts in service of the light.

What Is Ego?

Over the years, spiritual teachers have defined ego in many different ways. Some lean on Freudian psychology, seeing the ego as an integral part of the personality that can aid our development when properly utilized. Some use the word to describe the lower aspects of the self. I think of ego as the part of us — whether that's a large part or a teeny tiny sliver — that wants to make our spiritual work into a performance. It's the desire to get involved with what's happening and take credit.

The way I see it, our spiritual gifts are exactly that: gifts, given to us by a benevolent Source who intends us to use them for the highest good of all involved. It's up to us to become conduits. We cleanse and ground (as explained in the introduction) so that we can become clear channels, with as little personal involvement as possible. Our ability to channel, to communicate with Spirit, to follow our intuition, is not a reflection of us or our worth — on the contrary, our worth in the eyes of the divine is unchanging. This is simply the service we have been asked to perform. It's not about us at all.

As humans, we can easily become confused. We can begin to think that we *are* our gifts, that our very value as human beings is reliant on how we *perform*. When this is the case, our performance becomes very important to us, because we have something to prove.

This can happen at a major level or a minor one. Ego can show up in a one-on-one conversation with a friend as easily as it can in front of an audience of hundreds. One moment we're totally in the light, in gratitude for all we have been given and happy to put our gifts into service. Then we get somewhat lost in that happiness. We start off marveling at how incredible the spirit world is, then we extend that sense of wonder to our Team. These are good things! They mean we're on the right track. We take a wrong turn, however, when we turn that delighted admiration toward ourselves, in the mistaken belief that we are somehow responsible for what's taking place.

A healthy sense of self-esteem is important. Spiritual lightwork, in most cases, contains a lovely fringe benefit of increasing our self-esteem, in part because we connect with our purpose. We feel good about ourselves when we're actively doing the things that we know we came here to do.

The difference between legitimate self-worth and an unchecked ego is razor-thin. That's part of what makes this work so tricky. We can primarily rely on our felt sense to determine the difference. There's something that just *feels wrong* when ego is in play. This sense takes time to develop, though; it isn't always easy, especially at the beginning.

It *is* beautiful to make a connection with Spirit. It *is* incredible to live a guided life. And each one of us is valuable, beautiful, and worthy. Yet being psychically gifted doesn't give us that worth, because we always had it. Choosing to work with our gifts is admirable and important, but it doesn't make us better than anyone else.

It helps to focus on getting ourselves out of the way. This can be a little scary, because it means we don't get to control things — or even to tell ourselves that we do. For instance, I have a strong commitment to helping people. It is my desire to help people connect with Spirit and to deliver messages from the Other Side. When my ego tries to elbow its way into the picture, it wants to take that a step further by controlling all the details. It wants to help *exactly this* person in *exactly that* way. My job, then, is to keep it in check by releasing any say over the details of who I help or how I help them, because at my core, I know what I really want is to help people in the manner in which Spirit thinks I should be helping people. I know that things work better when I surrender control. Note that this doesn't have anything to do with the size of the audience or the breadth of the platform. I've heard other psychics say that operating on a large platform is about ego, and I vehemently disagree. I feel that if Spirit guides us to offer our gifts to the masses and we refuse, that's ego, too — because, once again, we're getting way too involved in the details.

Backing off from those details requires trust. We have to trust that what we have been shown through guidance is correct, that we're in alignment, and that even when we don't fully understand the bigger picture, we're acting in service of that guidance. Yes, we are spiritual beings. We're human, too, though, living a human experience, and everything is being revealed to us in Spirit's time. That includes ego itself. As we climb through successes in our lives, small or large, ego is going to come in at some point — and when it does, we ask our Team for help, and we act on what they say. That's our role in the process. All we can do is play that small role, trusting that it is exactly what it should be.

It's OK if you don't feel that trust yet. It's also OK if you feel it sometimes, but other times your trust is shaky. The more you do this work, the more opportunities you have to build trust. As you learn to identify when your ego is acting, you'll get to practice releasing it over and over, surrendering to the greater process.

How Ego Shows Up

There are several main ways we can recognize that our ego is acting.

The first has to do with false self-worth. This has two facets. It can appear as bravado, which is the way many people think of ego: a haughty, self-important sort of pride, which at its root is desperate for approval. We've all seen this before. It's the thing we worry about when considering sharing our gifts on a large scale, because it's stereotypical — that arrogant, pompous person strutting around a stage before hundreds and channeling the dead. I promise you it's not the size of the audience that matters here; it's the ego.

There's a flip side to this. When a reading doesn't resonate, a psychic prediction doesn't come true, or the audience is too small, ego presents itself as something more like shame. Ego shows up as *My readings aren't good enough*, or *If I say something, it's going to be wrong*. Fear of judgment from others enters in here, because when the ego plays into shame, outside approval and inner worth are erroneously linked. Just like its prideful counterpart, the insecure, shame-ridden manifestation of ego keeps us from doing our work, too. Our development remains halted, unmoving, because we're too afraid of our own ego to risk being wrong.

Both of these are manifestations of *false* self-worth. Real, authentic self-worth is largely unaffected by the opinions of others.

My friend Lilian isn't on the psychic path but knows this struggle well. Every time one of her professional peers gets an award or receives some other accolade, she grapples with envy, feeling poorly about herself and what she is not accomplishing. Many of my students have had to work with this form of ego, too. For instance, Katelyn has been coming to my classes for years, and she knows that spiritual lightwork is her path, but her sense of insecurity is so strong that she's unable to work with her gift. She's full of book knowledge, but she can't trust her own abilities. She always feels like she's behind. Katelyn jumps between potential outlets for her gifts — she tried healing, writing, working with children — but she never fully manifests her psychic nature. Every time she pursues a direction, someone else comes along to demonstrate what success looks like in that arena. This should be a good thing, a source of inspiration for Katelyn! As I see it, her Team is sending these people to show her where she's headed. Instead of looking at that as a reflection of herself and what she's capable of, Katelyn is reminded of what she hasn't yet achieved, and she shuts down again, thinking she needs to gather more knowledge before proceeding. She'll never get there while she's completely consumed with what everybody else is doing. Meanwhile, she's a very talented psychic medium; Spirit is just waiting for her to figure that out.

Another way ego can manifest is in the form of chasing something. We can chase our own success, setting higher and higher standards for ourselves, or chase someone else's success instead of trusting that our Team is guiding us to exactly the right place. Ego can really mess with us when it comes to accomplishments. It wants a blue ribbon, every time. This is even more true if the person next to us got a blue ribbon; suddenly, we need it more than ever.

I'm a naturally competitive person. I played sports as a kid before moving on to a career in retail, where I was taught I was only as good as my last sale. Looking back, I can see that there was a bullying aspect to my sales career; I was bullied, and I learned to bully myself as a tool to push myself forward. It's taken a lot to undo this conditioning, but today I find my competitive tendencies helpful because they show me when my ego needs to be checked. The moment I feel that sense of competition coming on — with someone else or with myself — I know my ego is at work.

Trying to dictate the matter of timing plays in here, too. Our ego can trick us into thinking that we need to get things done in a certain time frame — that it's up to us to have this or that done in a predetermined amount of time or to align with a certain milestone in our lives. Perhaps we want to have reached a professional level by the age of thirty, or we want our family to be in a certain configuration when we're forty. Maybe we want to get a new business up and running in six months. In truth, it's trusting the timing of the universe and going with the flow that leads us to the best outcome every time. The rat race is in the realm of ego, so just set it aside. If we're shaming and judging ourselves, thinking there's somewhere to be other than exactly where we are, we can know for certain that our ego has taken over.

Finally, let's look at how ego can show up in us through mirroring other people. We often become very conscious of our own ego when we are around another unchecked ego. Our Team knocks on our door by sending such an ego in our direction, and in response, our own ego activates to show us where we need to work. This is delicate, because we are still always accountable for our ego — being in the presence of a bigger, more out-of-control ego does not let us off the hook for our behavior — yet we can take these experiences as lessons without continuing relationships with people who bring out the worst in us.

I've had to shy away from other mediums in the past when I perceive an activation in my own ego. My competitive nature rises, even if it's only inside my head, and I feel the stress of trying to keep up. That's *my* ego, and *I* am accountable for it, yes — but why is it activated? Sometimes the answer is simply the proximity to another out-of-control ego. If it's safe enough to gently call the other person to attention, I do this. I try to help. But in other cases, I feel like it's going to be toxic. I thank my guides for directing this person toward me, for showing me where my ego needs a little tune-up, and then I ask them to clear the space. I ask that the other person be well, be happy, find success, and love their life — and I ask that they be removed from mine.

This happened in a pretty major way when I gave a reading to a talented but relatively untrained healer. My guides quickly zeroed in on his healing abilities, so I shared aloud that he held strong potential that was worth developing. His ego went a bit berserk with this information. As it turned out, he'd long harbored another dream: fame.

Instead of investing in more training and developing his skill set, he began to position himself as a public personality. This would not have been any of my business, except that I started hearing from others that he was leaning on the reading he did with me as justification — essentially, he was boasting of an endorsement I hadn't offered. This activated me in a way that didn't serve my soul's purpose. I felt uneasy and wasn't sure how to respond, and I watched myself begin to react to the pressure by falling into old habits like insecurity and people-pleasing.

I asked my Team for help, and they encouraged me to pull back from the relationship ever so slightly. I did, and sure enough, they cleared the space; he stopped contacting me. I was left to sort through my own spiritual questions, to understand my actions in the relationship, parsing through how it triggered me and what role I played. It was a difficult experience, but it left me with the strong conviction that I know what is right and wrong for me, and while a little bit of ego activation can be instructive by showing me where to work, I don't need to surround myself with people or situations that push my ego to its edge.

When ego shows up, it's up to us to be accountable for *exactly what is ours* — no more, no less. Ego often pushes us to not hold ourselves accountable for our own actions. On the opposite end of that same spectrum, ego can try to convince us that we *should* be accountable for things that are quite frankly none of our business, like the approval of others, the timing of events, and the details of how they unfold.

As we begin to regularly check our ego, we see that the entire universe is waiting to support us. Our Team loves it when we question ego, because it's showing us what our soul was placed here to learn. It's revealing where and how we need to work. The effects of this work ripple out through our spiritual lives, too. Every time we knock our ego into the back seat and insist on letting our Team drive the bus — and *especially* when doing so requires a lot of effort — it's a small victory.

Three Ways to Work with Ego

So how exactly do we knock the ego to the back seat, check it at the door, or otherwise brush it aside so we can continue forward with our spiritual lightwork? I've found three methods to be most effective. They work right in the moment, as soon as we recognize that our ego is messing with us. I haven't presented them in a particular order; any of the three can work, anytime you need them.

The first of these is gratitude. When we express gratitude for the abilities we have been given, we immediately signal that we know our place in things. We send out a loud, clear message that we are not our gifts but rather the conduits for them. This can come in the form of a simple "thank you," either spoken aloud or internally. We can regularly express our gratitude to our Team for the guidance and wisdom they provide. It is also shown through our action. We can demonstrate gratitude by speaking of our psychic gifts and the work we do to develop them with reverence. And we can honor all the messages we receive, without question. Whatever input we receive from Spirit, no matter how random it may seem, we can trust it. Doing so shows that we're grateful and ready for more.

The second way to check our ego is to surrender our expectations. This starts with letting go of the time frame, which as I noted above, is one of the ego's favorite ways to pop into our spiritual discourse. When we set expectations on timing, telling the universe it's up to us to figure out exactly when everything is supposed to happen, our ego is in full force. It's easy to turn this around, though, because we can simply release the need to know *when*. This simple step has a major impact.

A quick sidenote on expectations: There is a clear difference between expectation and hope, and I would never want anyone to read this and confuse the two. Hope is better than expectations. It's higher; it goes beyond the realm of the ego and into the realm of Spirit. When we have expectations, about timing or anything else, we can lead ourselves to so much disappointment. But when we lean into the idea of hope, even if it's just a little pinpoint of light in the dark, it allows our vibration to immediately start to rise.

Expectations come with a need. Hope does not. And when we focus, even with total darkness around us, on the tiny pinpoint of light up ahead — the light of hope — there's no disappointment. We either arrive in that light or we keep hoping for it. Hope never fails. While it's important to surrender our expectations, don't misunderstand me here; definitely keep hanging on to hope.

The third way to disarm the ego is to focus on celebrating others' success and growth. I don't mean just to do that when you have to — I mean to make a point of it. Lift up your friends. Honor your teachers. Get excited about what your peers are doing. Do it consciously and consistently. I absolutely recommend you start practicing this now and continue throughout your journey with this book. We'll look at the power of celebrating others again in the final chapter, when it helps unlock your highest spiritual potential.

When we question the ego, we question scarcity. The ego wants to tell us that things like success, love, accolades, and spiritual growth are finite, and that there's only enough for the lucky. Then it suggests we might want to shove everyone else out of the way to ensure we are the sole recipients of such luck. This is all a farce — just lies, from start to finish. Don't fall for it. The universe is inherently abundant; there is enough good stuff to go around. And I'm not the first to say it, nor will I be the last, but it is a universal truth that spreading the love makes it grow.

When I celebrate other psychics — be they students in training, peers enjoying new levels of success, or people who seem to be a hundred miles ahead of me in terms of their gifts and development — my ego shudders, because it knows I've got its number. The ego is highly intelligent, and putting my attention toward the achievements of others is the quickest and easiest way to outsmart it. As an extra challenge, I have to do this *without beating myself up* in order for it to work. In fact,

I have to do it without comparing them with me at all. This isn't easy, especially when we've been taught to compare and compete.

Try it out. Envision someone you admire, or perhaps even envy, receiving praise in a way that activates your ego. See yourself responding with "I'm so happy for you." Try to mean it, with absolute gratitude for the exact place you are because it's the exact place the universe put you. Then let yourself be excited, because you can know that your Team is taking you there — not to that exact version of success, perhaps, but to *your* best version of success. If you want, you can even thank the universe for that preemptively: "Thank you for showing me the reflection of my own accomplishments, even before I have achieved them."

These three fantastic methods to work with the ego — expressing gratitude, surrendering expectations, and celebrating others — are available to us anytime we need them. I often find myself activating them right in the moment, as soon as I feel that little twinge that tells me ego is acting up.

Sometimes it helps to augment them with a more intentional practice to understand what's going on with our ego at any given point in time. The next section offers one such practice.

PRACTICE

·· ☽⊙☾ ··

Chakra Realignment

To do this practice, you'll need a notebook, a pen, and at least twenty minutes of uninterrupted time. Feel free to use candles, crystals, music, or whatever else you'd like to set the space for this exercise. Before you get started, I'll explain what the chakras are and how they work.

There are seven chakras, or energy centers, running up the body, each emanating a certain color: at the base of the perineum (red), in the low belly (orange), at the solar plexus (yellow), at the heart (green), at the throat (blue), at the third eye (violet), and at the crown of the head (white). The word *chakra* comes from the East, where it means "wheel," but similar wisdom has been echoed by many ancient cultures from around the world, suggesting that there's a shared understanding of the body's energy centers. Like wheels, these energy centers are meant to spin at a regular, even speed.

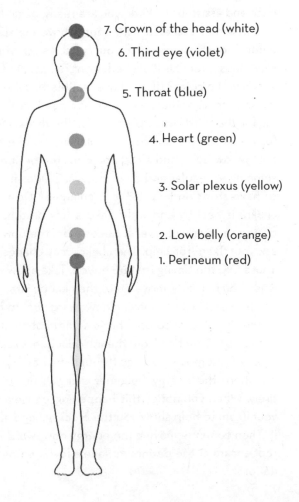

7. Crown of the head (white)

6. Third eye (violet)

5. Throat (blue)

4. Heart (green)

3. Solar plexus (yellow)

2. Low belly (orange)

1. Perineum (red)

As we pass through the challenges and other experiences of human life, the energy from our chakras can become blocked. We might psychically experience those blocks as colors, sensations, images, vibrations, or sounds or through other sensory input. When you perceive a block, *trust that perception*. There's no harm in doing so, and this practice is an important way to start working with your intuitive knowing on a deeper level.

We'll start with a very simple meditation. First, cleanse and ground. Then set your intention for your chakras to show you where your ego is most active. Gather your Team by asking for their presence and assistance. When you are ready, begin the meditation.

Imagine a universal light energy hovering above you, and let it enter through the crown of your head. Assess your seventh chakra. How does it feel? Is it aligned, front to back, left to right? Can you visualize the color? (If you have trouble visualizing the color, imagine something of that color, such as a pearl for the crown chakra, an iris for the third eye, a bluebell for the throat, the deepest jungle for the heart, the sun for the solar plexus, the fiery sky at sunset for the low belly, and a red apple for the perineum.) Is the chakra spinning at regular and even intervals? Does it continue smoothly or have stops and starts? Is it enlarged? Do you sense that this chakra is healthy and well? Take a few breaths and ask that this chakra receive whatever it needs from the universe. If necessary, ask your Team for help. The chakra may change or stay the same. That's OK; the timing isn't up to you. Take a few more breaths, and when you're ready, move on to the next chakra.

Proceed in a line moving downward, first to the third eye, then to the throat, and so on. This is somewhat similar to the Bringing In the Light practice from the introduction, except in this case, instead of just moving energy through the body, you're also focusing on where the energy becomes sluggish or stops circulating entirely. When you notice this happening, pause and breathe, asking your Team to help show you the blockage and, if possible, remove it. Then continue moving the energy downward until it meets your root chakra at the perineum. Take a few breaths to close the meditation.

When you're ready, get out your notebook or a journal and pen for an automatic-writing exercise.

Automatic writing has a long history. There are very famous mediums from all over the world whose primary method of spiritual connection is through writing. And while that may or may not end up being true for you, automatic writing is an excellent tool for everyone, because it demonstrates the power of getting out of the way and just letting the words flow. As you write, you may notice that your handwriting changes; resist the urge to correct it. You may find vocabulary or phrasing on the page that you rarely use in real life — in some cases, people might even use words they don't know and sometimes even languages they don't speak! While those are extreme examples, most people feel some degree of surprise when reading their automatic writing back to themselves out loud. You may be shocked to realize, as many students have remarked, "That just isn't *me*. But it's so true, at the same time." This is exactly the experience I want you to have!

Close your eyes and ask your guides, "What are these blocks, misalignments, and so forth trying to show me? Which chakra is offering me an opportunity for spiritual growth?" If you want, you can phrase the question in your own words and write it at the top of the page.

Start writing. Let the words flow until they come to a natural stop. This should occupy at least a few minutes.

When you're done, take several minutes to just breathe silently. Then read your words back to yourself *aloud*. There's such power in hearing your channeled message spoken out loud!

Check It...and Keep Checking It!

To close this chapter, I have a final note on ego.

If we're doing our work, each one of us is working on ego nearly all the time. It's an ever-present, ongoing task, like weeding the garden or doing laundry. As a result, the ego conversation is a common one among psychics. One day I was

talking to my psychic friend Julie and lamenting about ego —
perhaps mine, someone else's, or something more universal.
(It's the same old set of complaints every time, isn't it?) Julie
looked right at me and said, quite directly, "MaryAnn, if you're
wondering whether your ego is in check, *it is*."

It took me a minute to process her statement. She didn't
mean it was in check all the time. She didn't mean it would
forever be in check. What she meant was that in the exact moment we're wondering "How is my ego doing?" *it's doing fine*.

I've come to realize that this is true, so I teach it. One of
the best ways to keep our ego from taking over is to constantly
check in with it, because the very act of doing so thwarts it on
a certain level. Checking in with our ego regularly isn't all the
work, but it's a lot of it. Our ego can't get that out of control if
we don't allow it the opportunity to do so. Making this very
simple act into a habit signals a sea change in our spiritual development.

Checking our ego is the first technique that releases the divine secrets living inside of us: the truth of our own psychic nature that is always available to us, waiting to be activated. In the
next chapter, we'll look at the second technique. Like the first,
this next technique — learning to work through fear — is part
of an ongoing process essential to our spiritual development.

Chapter Two

HEY THERE, FEAR!

Addressing What Scares You

Fear happens. It's unavoidable. It's part of what makes us human.

When fear rears its ugly head, it creates havoc. Though this is never an easy experience, it can be particularly damaging for spiritual Lightworkers. Fear can cause us to question ourselves and lose confidence in our intuitive abilities or the messages we have been asked to deliver. This then puts a lid on the goodness we can spread. Our gifts are meant to be shared; they don't do well when bottled up. A blocked gift can turn into a lack of purpose or a latent sense of anxiety, both of which produce even more fear. The cycle continues.

Or, at least, it continues until we choose to stop it.

Like checking our ego, putting a stop to our fear isn't a

onetime thing — it's a lifelong practice. Luckily, it gets easier as we go along. When we learn to address fear right away, regularly checking in to assess its role in our decision-making, it becomes easier to integrate fear work into our spiritual development process.

Fear is closely tied to ego, because fear is often one of the ways ego speaks. Caving in to either of these forces has remarkable power to block our psychic development, while working with both has an even greater power to propel us forward. Our human experience with both ego and fear dictates the level of spiritual connection we can attain. It's up to each of us, therefore, to figure out our own way to work with fear.

This chapter explains what fear is actually all about and what we have to gain by working with it. We'll also consider some of the common manifestations of fear for intuitives. Along the way, I'll offer a couple of tools to help you begin to work with fear more consciously. By the end, you'll be on your way toward a new relationship with fear: one that is both ongoing and continually empowering.

Why Work with Fear?

Some years ago, at a time when I was feeling a lot of fear, a vision appeared during my meditation.

I was working with the Temple meditation, which has been so helpful along my journey. (You'll get to try it for yourself in chapter 3.) In my visualization, I prepared to enter my temple. One of my guides, however, had other plans. He took me to a long corridor filled with doors. Then he opened one of them to show me what was on the other side.

As the door swung open, I saw two big black rats. I am afraid of rats to begin with, but these two were particularly horrifying and carried a dark energy. They were fighting each other, scratching and biting as they squealed, a mess of tails and claws and teeth. They paid no attention to me, and I watched them, transfixed and disgusted, until my guide closed the door.

At the end of the corridor there was a council room. I went in there and began speaking with my guides, asking them to explain. They showed me my own memory of the rats and told me that because I am afraid of rats, the rats had a lesson to teach me about fear. Then my guides asked me to imagine putting a piece of food on my hand and offering it to the rats as they fought. I imagined myself doing this and saw that if I fed them, they would stop fighting each other. They would move closer and closer to me to eat and become stronger with each bite. But if I left them alone, they would just continue to fight without me.

My guides explained that in most circumstances, fear is best left to fight itself. It would rather hang out with other fear. Everything changes if we offer to feed our fear, though. It's up to us to refuse to give our fear-rats food.

I've thought of this vision often. I love that my guides thought to show me my own accountability in working with fear, and I feel compelled to share it with you, too. Fear is an opportunity — an opportunity to go deeper on the path and be accountable for what's ours — or an excuse to run away and hide. I know what I choose. In seeing it as an opportunity, especially with this vision of the rats guiding me, I can be accountable for what's mine without falling prey to the ego voice that says I should be accountable for all of it. In other words, the rats have nothing to do with me. I didn't create them or make them fight — they were doing that behind the door before I ever showed up. The food, though, and the decision to offer it, is completely within my realm of influence.

This vision didn't come to me by accident. As I mentioned, it was a particularly fearful time in my life. I was up against fear of failure — something I thought I had conquered in the past but which was showing up in a whole new way for me. I had been asking for help from my guides in meditation and more casually throughout my day, trying to figure out my next spiritual move in difficult circumstances. My request was genuine; when my guides decided to show me what they did, I acted upon it by shifting my relationship with fear entirely. Perhaps this is why they chose that moment to reveal the lesson: my next move was to work with my own fear.

Our guides are always ready to help us recognize the lesson. We have to do our own work to be ready to receive it. We have to be willing to accept what they offer and act upon it. To face fear completely, therefore, we need to have already faced the fear of what we might see in the mirror. We need to be willing to understand our participation in the challenges we face.

I like to think of this willingness as leaning into the lessons. When we lean into the lessons, we immediately start clearing space for what's bothering us to be resolved. Sitting with our own discomfort is part of spiritual growth. Working with fear consciously forces us into that discomfort, which is part of why it's so valuable. Then, instead of shying away from what arises, we can lean into it, asking our guides to show us whatever it is that we're meant to be learning. We can do that in passing; we can do it in meditation; we can do it in writing; we can chant it aloud. It doesn't matter how we ask; our guides *will* answer. When they do, the answer they give will have everything to do with our spiritual growth. It will show us where we need to work next — with fear, and beyond it.

Understanding Common Fears

There are many common fears associated with psychic development.

Some people wonder whether there is something morally wrong with communicating with Spirit or receiving guidance from our Team. This question often comes from people with strong religious backgrounds. I want to tread carefully because I haven't experienced this question myself; I've heard it from many others, but it has never arisen inside of me. As I've mentioned before, my mother was meditating and taking classes to help her channel way back in the 1970s, so I didn't ever form ideas that would tell me there was something wrong with spiritual lightwork. I didn't come to religion until adulthood, when I decided I wanted to take Communion and began catechism classes. Today, I am a confirmed Catholic, and I still don't feel friction between my moral center and my spiritual truth. I take the pieces of Catholicism that call me and integrate them into my work, no problem. I am not worried, because I know I am right with God.

The thing that allows me to do this — the thing that I want to impress upon you today — is the firm belief that I have a direct line to Spirit (as do you!). I know that if I'm being guided to be a medium, it's God's will that I be one. Those who aren't supposed to work with their psychic gifts *are not called to work with their psychic gifts*, plain and simple. This question comes up in nearly every workshop I teach, and it certainly comes up with many of my students in our one-on-one meetings. Every time, the answer is very straightforward: If your intuition is guiding you to continue this work, do it. If that weren't the right thing for you, you wouldn't receive guidance suggesting otherwise. Don't take it from me, though. Ask your own intuition and trust the answer when you receive it.

Another common fear is of dark energies or beings. On the altruistic level, no one wants to pass around something nasty, and on the very selfish level, that stuff is scary. I'm not going to tell you such things don't exist. Early in my development as a spiritual Lightworker, and especially before I began to work with my gift consciously (when my guides were trying to wake me up to my own potential), I had several unnerving experiences with things I didn't want to see. Yet our task is always to find the positive interpretation — the greater reason we sensed such energy. Sometimes Spirit shows us some of the darker stuff so that we can recognize the light. To a certain extent, our relationship with this icky stuff lies within the realm of boundaries, which we'll tackle in the next chapter. I know it causes a lot of concern, though, so let's first look at the fear these darker energies can trigger.

For the most part, psychic mediumship doesn't involve floating, transparent, ice-cold ghosts. It doesn't involve disembodied voices hovering in the air. As a bona fide psychic medium, I promise you that though these things happen, these versions of Spirit are usually rare and fleeting. The few times I've seen an apparition, it's been very fast, like a glitch in the frame. And while I've thought I heard my name called or someone knocking on the door, it's an inner hearing, not something I might confuse with the act of a living human. There have never been icy fingers gripping my shoulders or scary voices whispering cryptic warnings in my ear. As far as I know, even within the world of psychic mediumship, most of that creepy stuff still fits firmly into the *Ghostbusters* category of Hollywood invention.

If this stuff is rare, then why are we so worried about it? Once again, I'll assert that each of us is accountable — this time, for what we focus on and what we don't. One of my students, Rebekah, was watching another psychic do an Instagram livestream. The psychic answered questions one by one. One of the questioners was really strange; Rebekah thought he had a weird energy, and she immediately felt pulled to get offline. She closed the livestream, but she still felt funky afterward, like she just wasn't herself. She told one of her friends who is also a developing psychic, and the friend suggested that Rebekah had somehow taken in this other man's energy and it was invading her space. Rebekah was really disturbed by this. The more she thought about him, the more she could feel this man's energy. It was as if he had spiritually slimed her.

We met several days after the livestream. Still bothered by the experience, Rebekah asked me what to do. Maybe she thought I would tell her to smudge herself or something — and sure, if you see something that freaks you out or someone else's energy spiritually "slimes" you by leaving you with a heavy feeling, a little sage can't hurt. Feel free to smoke out the whole house! But I also told Rebekah that this was *her* issue, and it had nothing to do with the other guy. The other guy was what he was — maybe weird, maybe negative, whatever — but he didn't jump through Instagram to psychically attack Rebekah. Instead, she felt fear, and then she spent the next few days feeding it. As she thought about this person who felt negative to her, she herself became more and more negative, and yeah, that brought more nasty vibes her way — how could it not? He didn't slime her; Rebekah slimed herself.

Is there dark stuff out there? Yes. Do some people practice mediumship in a negative way? Absolutely. Can that energy feel slimy, nasty, icky, and the like? You bet. We're allowed to feel dark, heavy things; sometimes the world is dark and heavy. Our response is everything, though. Like my guides demonstrated with the rats, we can feed that energy or just let it fight with itself.

When all else fails, we can ask for help, too. There are many ways to do this. We can call on healing energy in the form of light. We can call our spirit guides, angels, and loved ones to come to our aid. We can ask for a dream or a vision to help clarify the guidance we receive. We can put pen to paper, ask Spirit to send us a positive mantra, and spend a few minutes chanting it aloud. All these techniques reaffirm that we are Lightworkers in service of the highest and best energies, and that lets the whole universe know what kind of input to send us in the future. Our Team is always happy to help us get out of the slime cycle.

Sometimes, even when the universe is sending the highest and best, we can still get hung up on the cynical reactions of the people around us. This is another common manifestation of fear. Navigating relationships with skeptical friends and family members can be difficult, and people who read for others will find many cynics who enjoy playing "stump the psychic" in an attempt to prove their belief that communication with the Other Side is not possible. When this happens, it's important to remind ourselves that what others think of us is not our business. We've been called to work with our psychic abilities, so we do. If we're guided to deliver messages, we deliver them with kindness and grace. (More on that in chapter 6.) Being *believed* does not need to be part of our mission.

It took a while for me to figure it out, but I ultimately regained *so much energy* when I stopped worrying about whether people believed in my gifts. I'm a serious debater; when I was a kid, my father used to say I would be a lawyer when I grew up. I love to argue a point, and I'm pretty stubborn about it. Yet when I am serving as a Lightworker, none of it has anything to do with me. Being believed is not the reason I share my gift; I share it because that's what Spirit wants me to do. I am not the least bit interested in convincing skeptics.

Judgment from others is part of the game, regardless of whether we're psychic mediums. No matter what any of us do in life, someone is always going to come at us, saying we're wrong. At the same time, each one of us is accountable for doing our work in the world. The moves that Source energy desires for us are always the best moves for us to make.

If your Team wants you to go public with your psychic work, you'll likely be criticized for it by someone or other, but I also promise you that you will find your people. And if you are instead guided to connect with your Team frequently throughout your day, asking for personal guidance and acting on it immediately, do that — regardless of what anyone else thinks. This work is bigger than their judgment.

The more you speak the truth and your authentic voice comes out, the more you're going to not only believe it deep down within yourself but radiate that belief outward as well. A self-confident psychic *exudes* psychic energy. They completely own it. And a person who is in regular connection with their Team is automatically conferred that confidence. (Note that this is just a hairbreadth away from the bravado I wrote about in the previous chapter; there's that tricky ego again! The difference is that this confidence stems from authentic self-worth — the sense of inherent worthiness that doesn't come from the outside but instead arises from within.) When someone owns who they are, with total love and no apologies, either the people around them own it with them or they don't stay around. Those who leave are meant to do so; they are clearing space for a more aligned community to arrive.

The moment we stand up to this ego-based fear of being judged, criticized, and not believed, something relaxes in us. Then the whole universe steps up to take care of us. We can look for indications that Spirit is supporting us, such as an uplifting text from a friend or a sign from our Team. It comes nearly every time, encouraging us to bravely continue.

These are just some of the most common fears people have on the psychic path. All fear has something in common, though, which is that when we dedicate ourselves to the work of conquering it, the communication with our Team strengthens. In many cases, that in itself calms our fears.

In others, it triggers a new set of fears to face.

Fear of Success and Failure

Whenever we dedicate ourselves to a new pursuit, whether it's getting into shape or baking or painting landscapes, it's natural to want to be good at it — *right away*. This is also an ego thing, to a large degree. We want proficiency. We want a reliable skill that we can pull out and use when we need it. Yet, like most people who have ever tried to get into shape or learn to bake or paint landscapes will attest, it doesn't happen overnight. That gives us a lot of time to think.

This is when fear of the future comes in. What if we fail? Worse, what if we succeed?

This moment is pivotal, because the way we deal with these fear-based thoughts says everything about the degree to which they can govern us. It's easy to fall into a failure mentality because believing in success is risky; it carries the fear of disappointment.

This is part of the reason why I always encourage my students to dream as big as they want to dream but to focus on the action as much as the vision. I love manifestation work; I believe there's a whole lot we can manifest when we learn how to do it. Yet it still requires action. It requires us to put our free will toward creating what we want.

When we're quaking with fear of the future, we often focus on the idea that it's not going to work out. We tell ourselves that we aren't going to be able to contact our loved ones, that we aren't going to be able to read for other people — that whatever it is that brought us to work with our psychic gifts in the first place, we aren't going to realize that goal. In that circumstance, it often feels easier to play it safe and act small. Our action manifests our fear right into reality.

When this happens, we can lean into the possibility that it will work out — we just don't know how yet. We're showing up. We're pushing ourselves beyond our comfort zone. We're doing the work to develop our psychic gifts consciously, and where that road leads is not up to us, as long as it's grounded in light. This works on the flip side, too, for those who suspect they have significant psychic abilities and are afraid of what that might mean. I've seen a lot of students go through this, and I get it.

It can be hard to give up an identity. I spent most of my first marriage convinced I would never get divorced; I was convinced that my role was to stay home with my children and dedicate everything to their pursuits and whatever might be in their interests, including continuing my marriage with their father. The idea of being a wife and mother felt safe and secure. It was comfortable, and I didn't want to leave that. It was profoundly difficult for me to give up the very image of myself as someone who would never get divorced, just as adopting the mantle of psychic medium is terrifying to many of my students. Right in the middle of that process, somewhere between the dismantling and reinvention, my guides called me to start working with my psychic gifts. It's as if I dissolved completely and was rebuilt from the ground up. Spirit brought me the guidance and the people I needed to keep on going, so I did.

Many of my students experience this dismantling process. When that starts to happen, it can be uncomfortable, especially because there's no way to know how deep it will go. Take good care of yourself when you're feeling tender. Reach out to the people in your life who can help — including the new people you'll meet on the path, who understand what it's like to go through a spiritual transformation. These people *will* come. One of the most beautiful aspects of working with developing psychics is seeing how supportive and positive my students are toward each other.

Part of working through fear involves being open to whatever arises. Ariela came into my classes carrying a lot of trauma. She'd had to contend with abuse, addictions, and self-harming behaviors for years. Spirituality helped bring Ariela out of her darkness, and as she began to connect with her version of God, she started receiving channeled messages. That's when she found me. At first, she was very nervous about what the other students would think of what she was doing — and I can only imagine that she was even *more* nervous about what the people at home thought! She had all this talent, but she played it small. As time went on, Ariela started racking up positive experiences in class. Time and again, her intuitive skills were confirmed. Each time she overcame something, she would become more confident. I watched her dive deeper and deeper into the spiritual world.

Suddenly, Ariela's channeling intensified tenfold. She started uploading her messages to YouTube, put up a website, and went all in. Today, her confidence is soaring! She looked at her fear, flipped it the bird, and kept going. I watch her videos, which are full of Spirit messages and love, and I'm so happy to see Ariela doing exactly what her Team wants her to do. I've been able to witness her healing through the process of finding success as a transmedium, bringing messages from another plane here to Earth. I've seen a similar phenomenon among healers, artists, and others whose psychic development morphed into something they never imagined possible. These students start with the methods I suggest, but then they turn it into a DIY process as their gifts develop. It's the best possible outcome, as I see it!

If you are someone who is afraid to develop your psychic gifts because you realize how strong they are, you are not alone — I feel you. This is a whole new world, and facing that can be overwhelming. Yet if your guides are pointing you in that direction, I think you already know you have to listen. You wouldn't be reading these words were that not the case. Look back on your life and all the terrifying things you have gone through. Acknowledge them, and then gently push your fear to the side. I'd never tell you to just sweep it away, but I encourage you to walk alongside your fear in parallel. You'll join the ranks of the many courageous souls who have walked before you.

PRACTICE

Chakra Realignment

This simple exercise uses the psychic version of the five-second rule. This means five-second answers are necessary; ask, and then jot down the first thing that pops into your head. I love using tools like this that strengthen our ability to tap into the psychic realm immediately. They're especially helpful early in the process of psychic development, because it can be so amazing to see how much we already *know* without having to work at it. That gives us the confidence we need to make the practice our own. As you work with it, be patient and have fun. It's meant to be light!

Start by cleansing and grounding. Signal to your Team that you're ready to receive their guidance.

Then get out a journal and a pen. Start by making three columns, labeled (from left to right) "Fear," "What I'd Do Without It," and "Mantra."

Write down your top five fears in the left column, leaving plenty of space between them. Do it quickly, without pausing to think too much. Just let your pen fly!

Then fill out the middle column. What might you complete, accomplish, or even *stop* doing in the absence of that fear? There may be a list of answers. Again, use the five-second rule for each, and let this flow freely.

When you've completed the middle column, take a moment to stop and breathe. Reconnect your energy to the floor, recommitting to calling the light in through your crown chakra. Connect and center yourself in whatever way works for you.

Now, it's time to turn each fear into a mantra. You don't need to use the five-second rule for this (unless the answer pops up naturally!) — even when I do this myself, it sometimes takes a minute to find a strong mantra. Your mantra should be affirming and in the present, not future, tense (phrased as "I am" instead of "I will," for instance). Here's one example:

FEAR	WHAT I'D DO WITHOUT IT	MANTRA
Leaving my high-stress job for a field that interests me	Enjoy my days more Have energy to develop my other gifts and skills after work Be open to the career path of my dreams Feel higher self-esteem knowing I am working in the right field	I deserve to expand professionally and achieve my dreams

As you create your mantras, you may find that you start to somewhat channel them. This is great news; it means the DIY aspect of this process is unfolding. Your Team knows how deep you are going in order to address your fear, and they may show up to help you out by whispering the right answers. If that happens, roll with it!

Once you feel content with your mantras, start practicing them. Some people write them on small pieces of paper and tape them around the house, repeating them aloud when they pass by. Others program reminders of their mantras into their phones or add their mantras to an existing meditation practice. This is your process, and I encourage you to do it your own way! The only thing that matters is that you work with your mantras regularly until your guides tell you otherwise.

Fearlessly Moving Forward

When all else fails, you can acknowledge your fear, thank it for being a part of your path, and kindly push it to the side. It's my sincere hope that the power of both the five-second rule and the mantra can help you recognize, once and for all, that *acknowledging* fear doesn't mean you have to *listen* to it. Fears often can't be prevented; for most people, they're part of the process. But whether they block you is on you and you alone.

If things get really tough and it seems impossible to do anything else, please keep cleansing and grounding. I promise that these practices alone can hold you through the most difficult times, because they allow your Team to come in and help you.

The best mediums I know have found a way to work with their fear and continue moving forward anyway. That is what allows us to develop our psychic abilities, getting into the higher-level work related to *how* and *when* we receive — and don't receive — psychic information.

Chapter Three

CLAIRS AND BOUNDARIES

Studying Your Psychic Structure

Once we're solidly addressing ego and fear and Spirit knows it's safe, our Team starts to play with us a bit. They initiate the dance, stepping forward to see if we step back, sashaying this way and that. Our guides also want *us* to initiate the connection. They've been loving, supporting, and guiding us all along, and they're always ready to communicate. After all, they're our very best friends. So they particularly love it when we reach out to begin the conversation. They respond enthusiastically.

This enthusiasm can be intense. Have you ever seen a meme or a video on social media that jokes about spiritual awakenings? I have seen quite a few that get at the same idea:

we often think that a spiritual awakening will be sweet and tidy, and it's usually, to put it bluntly, a shit show. I remember this clearly from my own life. It used to be that Spirit would try to talk to me at all hours of the night, interrupting whatever I was doing. I have come to realize that this is a common experience for spiritual Lightworkers, especially early in the process. The reason is twofold. First, our ability to perceive Spirit becomes sensitized, meaning we feel everything more acutely and immediately. Second (and this is especially true if we find the experience exciting, terrifying, or any other extreme emotion), our naturally sensitive, empathic traits open the floodgates between the world of Spirit and our own plane. Our vibration jumps all over the place, adjusting to meet the needs of others, and this is a profoundly destabilizing experience.

In the preface of this book, I told you quite plainly that doing this work will naturally decrease the urge to please the people around you. That is partly due to increased self-worth and partly due to the hard-and-fast boundaries psychic development causes you to form with Spirit. If you can set and maintain a spiritual boundary, you can set and maintain a human one — I promise.

The third technique I'm going to introduce, therefore, is all about managing the type and amount of spiritual input we receive, continually adjusting it to meet our needs. That starts with figuring out our *clairs*, or the six ways Spirit can communicate with us through sensory input. Then we have to learn how to set clear boundaries and maintain them. This chapter leads you through the process.

Our Psychic Senses

Each of us has a different relationship with each of the six clairs. Many people begin this work expecting to immediately develop *clairvoyance* (the ability to "see" Spirit through imagery) or *clairaudience* (the ability to "hear" Spirit speaking aloud). While some people possess these abilities, others will work more easily with one of the other four clairs — *clairsentience*, or the ability to physically feel Spirit; *clairalience*, which allows us to smell what Spirit suggests to us; *clairgustance*, which brings our sense of taste on board; or *claircognizance*, which taps into our sixth sense and allows us to just know things without being aware of how or where we learned them.

CLAIR	PHYSICAL SENSE	EXAMPLES
Clairvoyance	Seeing	Flashes in the third eye, visions, auras, colors, symbols
Clairaudience	Hearing	Voices and sounds in the inner ear, repetitive thoughts
Clairsentience	Feeling/ sensation	Changes in temperature, pressure, texture
Clairalience	Smelling	"Phantom" smells such as smoke, death/rot, flowers
Clairgustance	Tasting	Tasting metal, sourness, sweetness, spice
Claircognizance	Knowing	A strong sense of what has happened or is going to happen, an unusually strong opinion

I remember the first time I realized I was clairaudient. It was early in my process of consciously connecting with the Other Side, and I had been struggling to hear Spirit. Though I knew I was picking up on something, I was still waiting to hear someone else's voice whispering in my ear. I imagined the experience would be monumental and obvious. Then my teacher said six simple words that have never left me: "Spirit speaks in your own voice."

Boom. I was instantly transported to dozens of past experiences where my own intuition seemed to come through verbally: "Turn left!"; "Don't book that trip!"; "Pull over! Now!"; "He's lying. Don't trust him!" I even thought back to the voice I'd heard as a teenager when watching a TV show about psychics: "You can do this." Though I had trusted the voice I heard, I had assumed it was mine; it was the voice of intuition, and isn't intuition all our own? For the first time I considered the possibility that my intuition was, and always had been, guided by Spirit. There wasn't some other voice to hear, and I wasn't missing out on something; instead, I'd been hearing my Team nudging me in the right direction all along.

Perhaps this version of clairaudience seems familiar — and perhaps it doesn't. As you develop your psychic abilities, you'll find that certain clairs are easier for you to connect with, while others are more difficult. That's OK; just like some of us are more athletic and others more bookish, our psychic gifts vary a lot, too. There's room for everyone in the world of psychic development, as long as we're all focused on channeling only the highest energies out there. So follow the ease; pay attention to what sense feels the strongest to you, and tap into that sensory experience to guide you.

You're also likely to undergo some degree of evolution in your experience with the clairs. Some psychics, for example, might spend a decade working with claircognizance before they develop clairalience and clairgustance, only to find that the smells and tastes Spirit sends quickly surpass the sense of knowing they spent so long developing. After all, it's normal for us to grow and change in the rest of our lives. Why wouldn't our clairs shift, too?

Since your clairs are somewhat of a moving target, automatic writing can be useful to get more in touch with them. Cleanse and ground; then sit down with a journal and a pen. Write "What are my clairs?" at the top of a page and, if you want, the name of a guide or loved one you'd like to ask specifically (you can also just ask your Team in general). Put pen to paper, and let the answer flow.

I experience all six of the clairs. (Remember Joseph, the pizzeria guy from the preface? He cut through a room of noise by coming at me with all the clairs at once!) I notice that I often tap into different clairs for different things — for instance, Spirit uses my sense of smell and taste in particular when I'm around illness. One of my earliest memories of being able to pick up on other people's energies occurred when my grandmother had colon cancer. I could smell the strong decay in her body, even when others couldn't, and experienced a metallic taste in my mouth. These sensory experiences immediately indicated to me that she was dying. (It was challenging for me, and I share more on this in the boundaries section later in this chapter.)

It would have been easy to brush off these experiences — maybe I ate something weird that left a metallic taste, or maybe something else in the room was giving off the smell of decay. A lot of people are waiting for their clairs to absolutely scream at them. They want lights to come down from the sky, and angels to descend from the heavens with trumpets and point to the answer. It's usually far more subtle than that. It doesn't take work to perceive Spirit, but it does take work to realize that's what we're perceiving, instead of rationalizing it away.

More often than not, this is particularly the case with visualization, which falls into the category of clairvoyance. One of my students, Jeanne, was doing a group writing exercise, and when it finished, she sighed. She announced that unfortunately the exercise had not worked. She had recently experienced several family losses and was desperate to connect with her loved ones on the Other Side, but she couldn't feel Spirit at all. I asked Jeanne to read back what she had written. First, she read back a clear description of herself walking through an alpine meadow filled with wildflowers. Then Jeanne read that she realized her beloved grandmother was walking alongside her. I stopped her and asked her how she knew her grandmother was there. "Well," Jeanne answered slowly, "I *thought about* her being there. So I saw her, but only in the way that you *think about* seeing something. I didn't actually believe she was there, because it wasn't actually my eyes that saw her."

Let me tell you this: if you see yourself walking in a meadow filled with wildflowers, and you *think about* seeing your beloved grandmother at your side, I want you to *actually believe she was there*. Yes, even if it wasn't actually your eyes that saw her. Turn to her! Say hello, and see what she says in response! I promise you that people who are not clairvoyant do not see things like that.

Consider how subtle this can be. Claircognizance can show up as intuition or a hunch. It can be that feeling that someone is standing next to you, even when there's no one there (don't worry; keep reading — I'm getting to boundaries next). Clairsentience can be goosebumps, the hair standing up on the back of your neck, the feeling of something crawling up your leg, or even the sensation of someone tugging at your clothes — I find that children who have passed often do this to get my attention. Clairgustance can be a sudden craving or an unexplained bad taste. Clairalience can be the wafting scent of lilacs, or powdered-sugar icing, or incense when there is no such thing around. It can be any unexplained smell such as cologne, food, or cigarette smoke. It can completely convince you someone just baked chocolate-chip cookies, even if you're on the beach. These can be fully realized experiences or the *suggestion* of an experience — as if, like Jeanne, you were suddenly *thinking about* having the experience or imagining you might. I've got a whole lot more on that coming up in the next chapter, but for now, all you need to understand is that the clairs can be much subtler than most people expect.

This is especially true of clairvoyance and clairaudience. For some reason, many people expect these two to be overwhelmingly obvious, perhaps even something they might confuse with input from the physical world. In truth, clairvoyance often comes in through a slideshow, suggestion, or memory. We might suddenly see a succession of red roses, or kinda-sorta-almost envision the outline of a red rose, or randomly think back to that time last summer we leaned down to smell a red rose, our field of vision closing in on the petals. Psychic vision quite rarely appears as an apparition or something that we might believe to be physically nearby. While that definitely can happen, it's uncommon.

Clairaudience can be tricky, too, because as I mentioned at the beginning of the chapter, many people mistake it for their own thoughts. In the weeks after I heard "Spirit speaks in your own voice," I began to realize that many of my opinions, as I stated in the preface, weren't in fact mine. It took time to learn to differentiate between what's really coming from me, MaryAnn, and what's clairaudient communication. Eventually, Spirit stopped coming in from both sides and started only speaking into my right ear. This helped immensely. Every once in a while, someone does give me a good shout if they really want to distract me, but most of the time, they send me somewhat audible thoughts from the right side of my consciousness, and this is enough.

In truth, many of us are channeling on a regular basis — we

just aren't doing it particularly skillfully. Our psychic feelers are open almost constantly, reaching out into the world for sensory input and tossing it back to us for processing. The problem is that we're waiting for the fanfare. We're waiting for a situation where we have no doubt, and that's impossible, because humans doubt by nature. To really figure out our clairs, we have to accept that they're most often mundane and subtle — especially because we've spent most of our lives squashing them down, pretending they aren't real. We have to first stop overthinking our clairs. Then we can start noticing the weird, out-of-place sensations that come up throughout an average day. That's when we can start understanding which of these sensory experiences are truly random and which are actually messages of a psychic nature. As we go through this process, our Team is cheering us along. They've been trying to reach us for all this time. Imagine their joy when we finally pick up the phone!

Once we become aware of how much psychic information we're receiving, boundaries become necessary — like, right now! Without them, overwhelm is assured. Let's look at what that means.

An Introduction to Boundaries

Boundaries is such a buzzword right now. Most teachers highlight the boundaries we set with other people, offering communication techniques and mentality shifts (such as my personal favorite, "That's none of my business") to help separate what we are accountable for in human relationships from what we are not. That work is important; as I've mentioned before, it's often a natural fringe benefit of creating psychic boundaries, because the methodology is more or less the same.

Just like you have boundaries with people, you get to have boundaries with Spirit, too. In fact, you *do* have boundaries, and you're setting them all the time with respect to what you allow and don't allow. So it's up to you to put your boundaries in the right place — and the "right place" is always the one that is enjoyable and sustainable for you, long-term. Spirit always encourages you to say when enough is enough. By doing these rituals, you say, "Open for business!" And that means when Spirit comes knocking and it's not the right moment, or you don't like the way a particular energy feels, you can also say, "Sorry, we're closed!"

Sometimes, as spiritual Lightworkers, we realize our psychic boundaries are either poorly maintained or set in the wrong place entirely. The most common way for this to come to our attention is through discomfort — either a bothersome onetime event, a series of such events, or a general sense that we just can't shake. For many empaths and sensitive people, this can show up as anxiety.

Anxiety can feel absolutely awful, and if you're experiencing it, my heart goes out to you. At the same time, I firmly believe that anxiety is a huge gift for empaths. It's a barometer to indicate where and how one's boundaries are working — or, more to the point, *not* working.

My clairs blew open as soon as I started my psychic training, and I began receiving energy from all directions. It was exciting and fun! I was so amazed by the whole process that I wanted to read for people as often as I could. This produced profound anxiety, something I had never struggled with before. It was extremely uncomfortable, almost debilitating.

Not only that, but there were really clear, tangible effects: I would walk into a room full of people and immediately get a headache, only to overhear someone a few minutes later complaining of the headache they'd had all day. This was particularly strong in the classes themselves, among the other students. We were reaching into each other's energetic space, trying to pick up on loved ones on the Other Side, and we ended up channeling our classmates' human emotions instead. All psychic training includes the essential work of learning how to be inside a certain energy without absorbing it — letting it be around us and perceiving it without being affected.

If we don't set our boundaries firmly, and if we don't make an ongoing practice of maintaining them, we're leaving ourselves wide open to whatever energy comes our way. And once word gets out that we're a wide-open portal to the physical human world, the amount — and sometimes the type — of incoming energy can have the effect of bombarding us with information.

When I first started reading for people, their grief would undo me and I would weep with my sitters. If someone else started crying, I would start to cry — and I was channeling their loved ones in Spirit, so people were crying pretty often. I learned to ask my guides to stop me from getting so emotionally involved, because I realized that having a wishy-washy emotional boundary like that could cause me to take in energy that wasn't mine, draining me. I see that happen to a lot of people in service professions — doctors, nurses, psychologists, and so on. It's important to remember that the goal of channeling Spirit is to be a conduit. We're not meant to absorb the energy or get ourselves involved. Doing so messes with the reading and opens up the possibility that we will mismessage by attaching personal experiences to the emotions we feel. We are of much more service when we get out of the way, despite the empathy we feel for the sitter, because the reading comes through more clearly.

After practicing this for many years, I now often tell people what's happening. "Please don't think I'm cold," I explain, "because I feel you, but I can't cry with you; I'll mismessage."

I consciously back off from my own emotional experience — not by suppressing it but, in the same way I address fear and ego, by nudging my emotions to the side and walking in parallel with them for a bit — and a sort of trance takes over. Within that trance, I can still access warmth, care, and humor, so I offer them freely, but I don't take anything on emotionally. It's just not the time to experience my own emotions or to let other people's flow through me — there are plenty of opportunities for that when I'm not reading. That is my protective boundary, and maintaining it is in everyone's best interest.

I won't predict death or illness. After accurately foretelling my grandmother's death, I told my guides I was done with that. They have respected my wishes — even when my sitters haven't! I once read for a woman who was in a miserable marriage. She hated her husband but felt financially and emotionally stuck, so she was afraid to leave. During the reading, she repeatedly asked me to tell her when her husband was going to die. I tried to redirect her, but she was insistent: she had to know if he was going to die soon, because she simply could not bear the drama of initiating a divorce. At some point, I broke into laughter because she wasn't even trying to sugarcoat how much she hated this guy and wanted him dead. She was so honest. Midway through the reading, she actually looked me in the eye and said, in a thick Brooklyn accent, "Can't you just ask Spirit to get rid of him already?" She was both joking and not *entirely* joking at the same time, and we both rolled with laughter to hear such frank, honest words slip out of her mouth.

Recalling this experience never fails to make me laugh again. Yet I also find it illustrative. To some extent, this sitter was just pushy, but I also believe she genuinely could not understand my boundary — she thought I could clearly see her husband's death but was refusing to tell her about it, when in fact my guides would never have shown it to me because it's not part of our contract. Eventually, I was able to transmit the only message Spirit gave on the topic: that her issue wasn't her husband but her own refusal to be accountable for what she knew she needed to do. If she hated him that much, she needed to either leave her husband or accept that she never would; according to her own guides, waiting around for him to die was not one of the options.

Ah, accountability. Do you notice how often we circle back here? This brings me to my final point about boundaries, which is that they also require accountability. In the previous chapter, I wrote about Rebekah, my sweet young student who felt she had been spiritually slimed via an Instagram livestream and proceeded to feed her fear for days over it. On a subtle level, Rebekah wanted to blame someone else for the way she was feeling. Being accountable for our own boundaries requires us to resist that urge. The wife who wanted her husband dead, on the other hand, was forthright about blaming him for her misery. Deep down, she probably already knew that she was accountable for the fact that she was remaining in the relationship — *I* know this, because her Team was loud and clear with me about that.

This doesn't mean we blame the victim; it's a subtle difference, and one that each of us learns over time. Psychic development, therefore, requires regularly assessing and adjusting our boundaries while still being 100 percent accountable for what's ours. It's tricky, delicate work. Let's look at how we can go about doing it.

Setting and Maintaining Psychic Boundaries

The easiest way to set psychic boundaries is directly: by telling the people around us where our boundaries are and doing the same with Spirit. For instance, in the example I gave a few pages back, I learned to set very clear boundaries around the amount of emotional engagement I bring to a reading, and I tell both my Team and the sitter where the boundary is. We can also set boundaries around the type of content we want to channel, such as the line I drew excluding illness and death. The same method works with "on" hours and "off" hours. We can state our hours of operation — when we're available for channeling and when we're not. We may have to defend these in either the psychic or human realm, but usually just firmly restating the boundary does the trick.

At the beginning, when I didn't understand boundaries, Spirit woke me up a lot. Nowadays, the only reason Spirit is allowed to mess with me at night is to tell me if I'm off-balance. When this happens, my Team usually sends me a dream to set me straight. They also know I'm off duty when I'm at the gym. No long-lost uncles by the free weights; no channeling chakra-alignment meditations on the elliptical. I get really into working out, and it is *not* a time when my clairs are open to receive messages! As a result, no messages come through — even though one time, a woman approached me in a spin class, my feet still pedaling furiously, and begged me to channel her loved one. I had to tell her quite plainly to back off.

Boundaries are all about finding that firm, kind line. And because there is always room for kindness, I find that my boundaries relax somewhat in certain circumstances, when it feels right. My boundaries are much looser with the energies of children and teenagers in Spirit, for example. The child I wrote about in the introduction was very persistent; he followed me from place to place, and I allowed that, just as I would naturally be less strict with a living child than I would with an adult. I find that children and teenagers are often persistent like this. It feels earnest, not pushy, so I generally allow it.

It can help to ask ourselves where, specifically, we want our boundaries to be so that we live a balanced life. Perhaps we will not channel or do a reading when we are around our kids. Perhaps we're wide open in the early morning, but we're off after dark. It could be that we don't want to deal with predictions or health or politics. You get to decide for yourself — only you know exactly where your boundaries need to be.

Once we decide where a boundary needs to be for any given situation and broadcast that to the universe, either verbally or energetically, it's up to us to maintain it. The main way we can do this is by respecting it. We have to keep to the schedule we set, only channeling when we're "on" and simply refusing to do so in off-hours. We must also have boundaries for our own energy, in both the human world and the Spirit realm. We can't be constantly giving ourselves over to others in need; we have to be sure our own needs are met first. When I started this work, it felt like I was exhausted all the time; I would get sick, I had chronic bronchitis, and I was just generally fatigued. This was compounded by anxiety. I had to pull back from the world energetically, protecting myself first.

While we're maintaining our boundaries, it's up to us to replenish ourselves. Self-care is so important to keeping our boundaries intact. We have to relax, enjoy ourselves, fill ourselves up with all the good stuff so we can stay safe while in service to others. I recommend reading books that have nothing to do with spirituality, exercising, listening to a favorite album or playlist, and napping at will. Keeping our boundaries healthy includes giving ourselves permission, now and forever, to rest and replenish consistently. It's part of our spiritual practice. As we rest, it can help to focus on our clairs and give attention to each of them separately, particularly the ones that are most dominant. Our clairs are replenished when we fill them with positivity and light.

For instance, if you're clairvoyant, you can go for a walk in the forest and feast your eyes on the beauty surrounding you. If you're clairaudient, listening to soothing music can give your spiritual ear a rest. If you're clairsentient, soaking in a hot bathtub or doing gentle yoga can work wonders. If you're clairalient, keeping essential oils in your purse for a quick pick-me-up may be the thing that saves you on a busy, social day. If you're clairgustant, intermittent fasting or seasonal cleanses can be very helpful (of course, you'll want to check with your doctor on what's best for your body). And if you're claircognizant, silent meditation can clear your head. As your clairs open and blossom, you'll find your own ways to honor them. Doing so will refill them with good energy, which is an important part of boundary maintenance.

In case you haven't yet noticed, boundaries are a whole lot of work. Luckily, our Team is always there to do the heavy lifting. We can elicit their help on the fly: when we're entering a crowded room, we can send our guides in ahead of us to clear the room of any energy that isn't there to serve the greatest good. We can do it casually, asking our guides to usher a certain person, idea, or energy out of our realm and leaving the details of how and when up to them. They'll always make sure this departure is in service of the light, so the only thing we need to do is ask.

In the next section, I'll offer a meditation to help you create a standing contract with your Team. This way, you can handle all the big stuff — on- and off-hours, restricted content, and so forth — all at once.

PRACTICE

…·)∘(·…

Creating a Psychic Contract

This is a specific meditation to set boundaries with your Team, helping them understand how they can best support you. It starts, however, with a much broader form of meditation called a Temple meditation. I didn't invent the Temple meditation or even channel it; it's a blend of similar meditations I've learned from several different teachers. Feel free to make it your own!

The temple is our own sacred place. It is of our own design, and everything is precisely as we would like it to be. We can go to our temple when we feel the need to retreat from the world and to get clear about our spiritual lives. We can also just go there to be there, because we like it. And we can go there to meet others, such as our guides and loved ones. It's not the only place where we can meet others, but many people find that it's a favorite because it feels so real.

If this is the first time you're entering your temple, add as much detail as you can. Don't worry about what you don't yet perceive; as you repeat the exercise, your senses will fill in the gaps. Over time, your temple will become as rich and detailed in your memory as your bedroom is today. This is part of why the meditation works so well.

You are welcome to use and repeat the first and final parts of this exercise as many times as you like, adapting the middle to fit whatever you'd like to do, ask, or see in your temple. Today, you're entering the temple for a very specific reason: to meet your guides and create a contract with them.

Creating a contract is like becoming the CEO of your clairs. It's up to you to decide when you want them on or off, what kind of content you want to come through them, why you want to use them, and so on. If you never take this opportunity, though, your clairs will remain stuck on their default settings. All you have to do is to tell your guides the terms of the contract, with love and respect for the support they give you; they are happy to comply.

This is a visualization meditation, so make sure you are comfortable. Read the entire meditation before beginning, or record yourself reading it aloud slowly and then play it back, if it is easier to "drop in" this way.

Begin by cleansing and grounding.

Then begin to envision a large hill in front of you. At the top of the hill is your temple. This temple can be as large or small, as ornate or simple, as you would like it to be. Make it your own! Put simply, it's just the most comfortable and wonderful place you would ever imagine. With each breath, you will ascend the hill.

Take your first step up the hill toward the temple. As you do, allow yourself to experience the color red, whether through visualization or through a felt sense. Breathe deeply.

Take a second step, allowing yourself to experience orange.

Take a third step, experiencing yellow.

Take a fourth step, green. Check in with the breath here; you're halfway to the temple, and it's important to breathe deeply.

Take a fifth step, blue.

Take a sixth step, violet or indigo. See the temple in front of you. You're still breathing deeply, and now you're nearly there.

As you take the seventh step, allow all the colors to fade into an iridescent golden white. In front of you, you see your temple.

As you approach your temple, the first things that catch your attention are the doors. Imagine these doors; see all the details, the colors, the textures, the size and shape. Then begin to take in the scene around your temple. See its roof and walls. What are they made of? See the surrounding gardens and landscape. Let your "seeing" be totally imaginative here, as if you are painting a picture in your mind's eye.

When you have seen most of your temple from the outside, bring your focus back to the doors. Perceive that they are opening, whether by your hand or on their own. When they are open wide enough, walk through them and into your temple. Take in the surroundings. Notice what the inside of your temple looks like, cataloging the size and shape of the room, all the colors and textures. If there is an altar, take note of what it looks like and perhaps what is placed upon it. You may want to offer something in your visualization — sage or incense or perhaps flowers.

Then look around. See all the lovely places to be in the temple — there may be furniture to sit on or just many cushions, a comfortable array of options for enjoying time in there. Set up two places to sit, facing each other, and take a seat in one of them. Ask a guide to come and sit in the other. You can invite a specific guide, if that option is available to you, or you can just generally ask for one of your guides. Take the chance — you may be surprised by who shows up! Trust whoever it is. This is your temple, you are cleansed and grounded, and light is flowing through you. This is the safest place you could possibly be!

When your guide arrives, greet them with joy. Thank them for their support. Then state the terms of your contract. As you do, your guide simply listens without interrupting; this isn't a negotiation or a debate. Be sure to create terms that you yourself can follow (if the rule is "no channeling at parties," you have to not channel at parties!). It's up to you to be very clear with both your guide and yourself. When you are finished, ask your guide to communicate the terms of the contract to all your other guides, and thank them again for their support before they leave.

Sit for a few minutes integrating this experience. Then prepare to leave the temple.

Turn and walk out the doors, allowing them to close behind you. Be present with the first color, that golden white, at the top of the hill.

Then take a step down the hill and allow the golden white to fade into an indigo violet. Experience this color fully.

Take another step down the hill, blue.

Another step, green. Check in with the breath.

Another step, yellow.

Another step, orange. You are nearly at the bottom.

Take the final step down the hill and allow yourself to experience red once more. Then take a few breaths, and end the meditation however it feels best to you. You may want to stretch, bow forward, or lie down.

If you feel called to journal about this experience or your contract terms, go for it! Know that you can return to your temple at any time to amend the contract as needed.

Strong Boundaries for Sharp Clairs

As we develop our psychic gifts, having sharp and perceptive clairs is important. These six psychic senses are our highest sources of input, providing us the information we need in order to interpret messages from other frequencies. We can enhance our ability to work with our clairs by knowing them well. We can also increase the flow of information we receive through them by keeping them highly sensitive.

Keeping our clairs sensitive without strong boundaries can be problematic, even dangerous. As our clairs become more fine-tuned, boundaries are the things that keep us grounded. They prevent the psychic overwhelm that can be bothersome at best, and entirely destabilizing at worst. Our boundaries are absolutely our responsibility; they are entirely within our realm of control. They are all our own, and we get to call the shots. Setting them clearly is the best way to keep ourselves safe and protected as we walk the path of spiritual Lightworkers.

There is so much to gain by doing so. We find that in the bubble of our own protection, with the support of our guides, the psychic realm is much more accessible. Our clairs can flourish, providing us with more and more information.

Once we have all that information, though, we need to know what to do with it. We need to know how to catalog and process the information coming in through our clairs using our existing frame of reference — our imagination.

Chapter Four

USE THAT IMAGINATION

Stepping into Your Role
in the Interpretive Process

Now that you understand how you can best communicate with Spirit and why it's essential to state your boundaries while doing so, the next technique helps you understand how to work through — not around — your own frame of reference to receive and interpret messages.

Once we start channeling energy and communicating with Spirit, it's common for us to begin questioning whether what we're sensing is simply wishful thinking — a fantasy, a dream, a figment of our wild imagination. I have news for you: *it is!*

The last chapter explained that Spirit communicates with us through our clairs. This mirrors the physical world, which communicates with us through the physical senses. It's just one example of how Spirit uses the unique abilities of our human bodies to get through to us. In addition to possessing senses, humans are also equipped to both store and process information — in other words, we possess both memory and creativity. Spirit can therefore access these faculties to help us make sense of the input we receive. Because we are individuals, each of us unique, Spirit can also take into account our personality to send a message especially for us — one that only we can interpret. And it can use familiar images that develop symbolic meaning to us. That means our nostalgic feelings, memories, personality, and symbolic understanding — what I call our *frame of reference* — are tools for us to receive spiritual transmission. Then we can enlist our imagination to connect the dots, creating context for the input we receive. We're not making it up, but we are filling it in.

The problem is that this filling in can be tricky. When the messages we receive from the outside are filtered through our own frame of reference, it looks and feels a whole lot like we conjured it from nothing. Many people have trouble trusting psychic communication that rests on their own imagination. This chapter is all about working with the imagination as a tool for psychic development. I'll describe how this works in greater detail, explaining the many ways this concept can unfold.

Spirit loves to find creative and interesting ways to use your frame of reference to send a message. Once you understand that, you'll be ready to start cataloging the signs and symbols you receive, creating a back-and-forth dialogue with Spirit. Then you'll take all this into one of my favorite practices, Meeting Hours in Heaven.

Working with the frame of reference, and especially the imagination, is the fourth technique I have to offer you. When you combine it with the preceding three, it will bring your psychic development to whole new levels. And, like all the other techniques, it works best when you make it your own.

Your Imagination: Use It or Lose It

The imagination is a powerful intuitive tool that Spirit uses as a blank canvas for imprinting information, images, dialogue, and other sensory experiences. We use these impressions when reading for ourselves or, for those who are called to read for others, for our sitter. In both cases, the ideas that come in are absolutely a joint effort between our brain and Spirit's communications. Spirit brings the content, but we fill in the blanks to create a felt experience that leaves a crystal clear imprint behind.

Manifesting is a great way to use our imagination, and it's one that many people have real-life experience with. Have you ever manifested something — whether it was something small, like a parking spot (my husband is great at that!), or something large, like a dream vacation? If so, it's easy to see the role imagination played.

Our imagination is so important, yet most adults rarely engage it freely. Somehow, we've confused an active imagination with immaturity, and this is unfortunate. We actively use our imagination as children, yet as we grow older, we discount its relevance in our lives. We may have even been scolded or shamed for using our imagination when we were "too old" to do so. Unused and unwanted, our imagination often atrophies; it retreats to a corner of our psyche, largely forgotten.

We have the ability to become aware of our imagination's relevancy and turn it on — similar to the clairs — or we can discount its role and nullify it. Think back to when you were a kid and how often you used your imagination as simply a part of your daily being. If someone gave you a stick, you could turn it into ten different things — a lightsaber, magic wand, conductor's baton, fishing pole... you name it. And it felt very real to have that imagined thing in your hot little hands, until someone told you differently.

The only way to get your imagination back is to start playing again. This is going to take time; don't expect it to all make sense right away. This is a recovery process. As you go through it, though, understand that the fact that your imagination is involved does not make the information you receive less "real" — on the contrary, some of the most "real" messages I have ever received contained lots of fill-in material from my own imagination.

Anytime Spirit uses our imagination to show us something, a certain alchemy is taking place. This is true even if we can't yet interpret the message we receive, because the very act of using our imagination, our soul's creativity, automatically raises our vibration. Children are usually very high-vibration beings; as such, they use their imagination all the time (and often — *ahem* — to talk to imaginary friends... just a little food for thought). It always serves us as adults to play with our inner child. Doing so helps us to connect.

Anything that spurs creativity brings you more into Spirit's realm. You need to first establish that mindset before you can interpret the messages your Team sends.

How the Imagination Unfolds

When you're an intuitive of any kind, Spirit is going to place images, thoughts, impressions, and other sensory experiences in your mind and throughout your body so that you can translate this to your sitter. When you use your imagination, it is actually Spirit working in collaboration with you to create the level of detail you're meant to communicate. Spirit is telling you what to say, do, or feel next.

This can unfold in a variety of ways. For instance, I once gave a young woman named Amanda a past-life reading. She was wearing a long-sleeved sweatshirt, so I was only able to see her face as I put her into a meditative state. I then walked her through a scene that Spirit provided for me — typically, this involves placing the sitter in a relaxing setting that's also relevant to their past life, like a meadow, a forest, a beach scene, a home, or other environment. For Amanda, Spirit told me to describe her walking down a long wooded pathway with lots of greenery around her. I described a dirt road that led to a wood-planked cabin with a charming porch and a rocker in the corner. I told her about a river nearby and could hear a wolf howl in the background. Eventually, I could see that she was relaxed enough to regress into a past life.

I then talked Amanda through a significant past life in which she had a happy but challenging experience in the wilderness. At the end of the reading, Amanda said, "MaryAnn, I'm so blown away. Look at this!" — and she unzipped her sweatshirt. On her arm was a full tattoo sleeve of the woods, just as I'd described in the meditation: the greenery, path, cabin, river, wolf — all of it! I had channeled her tattoo into the reading, and because I'd used such vivid detail to describe it, she could recognize the image. Once she did, trusting the past-life reading was that much easier — I mean, how could she even doubt it at that point? Using my imagination was the key. I initially saw the image in my mind's eye, but then I allowed myself to roll with it. If I had been afraid of how much I felt like I was "making it up," Amanda would have had a much less powerful reading.

It goes far beyond tattoos. If you have a good sense of humor, Spirit will engage that to interact with you. If imagery and metaphor come easily to you, Spirit will use a lot of symbols. Spirit may also use your own memories (for instance, the lake house you remember so fondly from your childhood might symbolize a happy family), your likes and dislikes (perhaps you'll think of chocolate cake when Spirit wants you to taste something delicious, or your favorite author will spring to mind to reference someone you admire), or spiritual imagery (you might envision saints if you connect with Catholicism, Hindu deities if you're more drawn to the yogic path, and so forth). These are just reflections of the meaning your imagination has already assigned to these ideas.

I invoke my imagination in all readings and communication with Spirit. I may be the one reading my client, but *Spirit* is using my imagination to pop images into my head — these aren't my thoughts, though I am typically asked to interpret them. So, I might see an apple orchard but then interpret what that means to me; all the while, Spirit has imprinted this image in my mind, also knowing full well what the interpretation is going to be. Spirit is always one step ahead of me. For instance, when I see an orchard, it's my symbol for a person who grew up near a farm, and even though it feels similar to a memory of my own because it lives in my mind, it's an image intended for someone else. Sometimes Spirit will use one of my own memories to relay a message as well. The day before a reading, Spirit will sometimes guide me to see TV shows, go to restaurants and other places, and meet people to create a reference for my client. I won't know it at the time — I'll simply think I happened upon these shows, restaurants, and strangers — but then Spirit will pop that memory back into my imagination during the reading.

As strange and unbelievable as it felt at first, I've come to understand that *of course* Spirit will work with my frame of reference, because it's an easy way to make sure I can interpret the message that's being given. That means if Spirit wants to show me someone whom I have never met, they may show me someone I know who carries some of their same personality traits or who shares their name. If Spirit wants me to conjure an experience that happened early in someone's childhood, often I'm shown my childhood house. This can be confusing at first, especially before you start documenting the signs and symbols Spirit is using to communicate with you as an individual (more on that later in this chapter). For now, it's enough to trust what Spirit is sending and understand that the messages you're receiving are real — you just may not know how to interpret them yet.

Take Keri (whom you met in the introduction), for example. Keri receives messages through writing, but early in the process, she often doubted herself and wondered whether she made them up. One day in class, her fears were put to rest. A name came to her, and she wrote it at the top of the page. Then Keri began to write about a person who had died. She felt that he was a young male, and she saw him standing near the beach and sensed that he was really sad. She could see that he had blond hair, a plaid shirt, bare feet — and that he'd killed himself. She also saw his mother start a foundation in her son's name.

The whole time Keri wrote about this, she hemmed and hawed and questioned herself, because it felt more like she was making the story up than channeling it. Finally, she read her writing to the class. When she finished, she turned to see that the woman who was sitting right behind her was sobbing. Keri had just perfectly described this other woman's son — down to his name, the way he died, and the foundation she had started in his name. What Keri thought she was making up was actually factual. From that day on, she gave her imagination the credit it deserved.

Even though I know all this and am accustomed to walking students through it, I'm still surprised by how imaginative some of my own channeled messages can be. I'll never forget the reading where I saw an elephant, followed by a daisy, and though my brain said it was too weird a combo to mention, my instincts told me that Spirit was using my imagination to convey a message. Sure enough, my client used to work in a circus, and she'd grown very fond of an elephant named Daisy! What are the odds of that?

Another time, I scheduled a woman with a common first name for a reading. During our appointment, I kept hearing her name over and over, and it brought to mind one of my favorite pop groups from the eighties whose lead singer had that name. Eventually, I told the client this, and I even sang the opening bars of the group's most well-known song, laughing as I remembered having the track on repeat during my teenage years. "Yep, that's me!" she responded. She was surprisingly enthusiastic about it. I laughed again, saying yeah, I knew it was her name — and that it wasn't a psychic thing, because I could see her first name on my schedule. "No, you don't understand; it *is* a psychic thing," she explained. "That's me. I was in that group. I'm the one who sang that song." Over the course of my life, I've probably met hundreds of women with that same name. Only once did I sing that song — and it was to the woman who performed it. Yet, had I gotten lost in the fact that I loved that song as a teenager, not considering it in the context of a reading, I would have never shared it with her.

Believing the imagination can be hard, but positive experiences like the ones I described above build trust. Still, some students continue to have questions about how this works with ego. If you're feeling unsure, consider this: In my experience, the ego is unlikely to send us incorrect or totally off-base messages. What's much more likely is that Spirit will send us a message and our ego will slip in to "help out" with the interpretation — in case you didn't catch that, the quotation marks mean that this "help" isn't very helpful — or tell us that what we're imagining can't possibly be right. For now, know that whatever you receive is probably real — even if you have no idea what it means. Yet.

Working with Signs and Symbols

As you become comfortable receiving input through your clairs and expanding upon it with your imagination, you'll be able to start interpreting what you receive. The primary way that I do this is through working with signs and symbols. I've got much more to share on how to use these in chapter 6, but for now, I want to introduce how they work.

Spirit often communicates metaphorically by using symbols — images or ideas that represent a larger meaning to the one who receives them. Symbols may also be signs, meaning they arrive at the perfect time and place to indicate the move(s) Spirit wants you to make. For instance, in chapter 2, I wrote about my vision of the rats. Rats symbolize fear for me personally; as I noted before, I am afraid of them. They were sent as a sign at that exact moment to show me I had something new to learn about fear.

Sometimes it's easy to interpret what Spirit sends. You may see a thermometer when someone is sick or feel tears well up when someone is grieving. In these cases, it's important to understand that the symbol only seems obvious because it's coming in through your own frame of reference, meaning illness and grief are the first things *you* would think of when you saw those images. Someone else might interpret those images differently. For instance, when Spirit wants to indicate that someone is trying to control the timeline of events to their own detriment, I am shown a clock. This interpretation seems obvious to me. But Spirit might show someone else a clock to mean something else entirely — for instance, that it's time to get moving on something, that time is running out, or that they need to wait for the right time. With just this one symbol, Spirit will send different messages to different people. The interpretation depends on that individual psychic's frame of reference.

This is why tending to your connection with Spirit starts with paying attention to your experiences. Notice the symbols you receive, as well as how you receive them. This will help you map the symbols Spirit uses to get through to you. I strongly suggest that all developing psychics, especially those working with mediumship or who want to read for other people, start developing a signs-and-symbols journal. This is a simple ongoing exercise wherein you write down what you saw and what it meant (even if it's just a guess!). It's important to keep track of this information as it evolves.

Some symbols are harder to interpret than others. I've seen some really strange things, and it can take a while to make sense of them! When this happens, the most helpful thing to do is to start asking questions. Ask yourself, *What does this symbol mean to me?* Ask your Team, whether it's through a meditation, through an automatic-writing exercise, or even through a request for another symbol to help clarify the message. If it helps, you can ask other psychics about their symbols, but don't rely too much on their interpretation, as Spirit is working with their frame of reference in one way and with yours in another. We can help each other a lot — indeed, community building with other psychics is deeply important in this process! — but trust your knowing, too.

When you land on the right interpretation for a symbol,

you'll know it. I've seen it happen hundreds of times. Take Jenny, who is highly clairalient, for example. She was walking through her house one day, not a flower or a scented candle in sight, when she smelled lilacs. Then it happened again. She wanted to know what was up. I asked her about lilacs, and she shared that they didn't have any particular meaning to her. She became quiet and I waited. Then I heard it: "... but ..." I know that "but." That "but" comes right before someone says something so intuitive, so spot-on, that it was almost certainly downloaded directly from Spirit. It turned out the smell of lilacs "kind of" reminded Jenny of her grandmother. I suggested that the next time she smelled lilacs, she could casually ask her Team whether her grandmother was around. Now, whenever Jenny's grandmother wants to communicate with her, she sends lilacs.

As you start to develop your own set of symbols, you can also start asking for them as signs. The idea of asking for a sign usually isn't new to my students; you, too, may have been asking for signs for a while. But doing so while using your existing bank of symbols brings it to a whole new level. You can even get really specific with this. If dragonflies are a symbol for you, ask for a green-and-orange one. Or ask for one in January, when the snow is falling outside and you've kicked back by the fireplace, not a live dragonfly to be found within a day's drive. Play with it. Wait for your green-and-orange dragonfly to show up, because it will — maybe as a meme someone sends you, or as the print on the bib you're about to buy off a baby-shower registry, or painted as a logo on the side of a truck. Spirit loves playing these games with you. It gives your Team great joy to answer these requests — the weirder and more specific, the better!

Receiving a sign provides a huge confidence boost. It lets us know our Team is always there. This makes it a great practice for developing self-worth! You can ask for a sign from a loved one who has passed, or you can ask for a sign to appear at the right moment to help you make a decision, such as a career or relationship shift. I always encourage a DIY approach, so play around with signs. If you want, you can even ask your Team what to make for dinner!

Working with signs and symbols will get you quick confirmation that your imagination isn't in the way but is actually part of the process. This is precisely the confidence you'll need for the next exercise.

PRACTICE

Meeting Hours in Heaven

Meditation is the easiest way to use your imagination for yourself and others. The first thing you can do is put yourself into a calm, meditative state and settle into your imagination. In this meditation, which I call Meeting Hours in Heaven, you'll imagine a familiar meeting place, using as many senses as you can, and then invite a loved one to join you in this space for a conversation. Like automatic writing, this exercise is a tool you can use for guidance whenever you want. You may do it just this one time, or you may repeat the practice over and over.

We can be completely, 100 percent ourselves with Spirit. Because Spirit shows up here as a loved one, Meeting Hours in Heaven reminds us that we can be unapologetically ourselves and have a comfortable working dialogue with Spirit's other forms, too. You'll naturally be yourself around your loved ones, and that way, when you meet spirit guides and/or angels, you can do the same, using your vocabulary, your intonations, your humor.

I always begin this practice with detailing the meeting place. When I was a kid, we used to go out to Southampton, Long Island, where my aunt owned a set of family bungalows. I visualize one of the bungalows: the rock pathway leading up to it, the smell of seawater, the creak of the screen door, the incredibly orange vinyl countertop in the kitchen, the paneling in the bedroom. Or I'll imagine my great-grandmother's house: the plastic covering the couches, the weeping-willow trees in the backyard, the laundry line strung between them, the smell of her Italian meatballs cooking. I create such a vivid scene that it feels incredibly real, like putting on a virtual-reality headset, and because it's a familiar place, it also feels safe. I watch the whole thing like a movie and wait to see who shows up — or, if there's someone in particular I'd like to connect with, I go to a place where that person felt comfortable and at home and where I feel very safe. I don't try to bring loved ones to my environment; I go to theirs. But I do it within my own frame of reference — I use a place where I have actually been — so my memory and imagination can make for a richer experience. It just gives Spirit more to work with.

It's also important to make yourself whatever age you'd like in this exercise. You can even find a mirror in your meditation to revisit what you looked like at the time. How is your hair styled? What are your clothes like? Here, if I'm using my great-grandmother's house, I picture myself as a young child. I see myself moving through the gate of the picket fence, crunching on the gravel in her circular driveway, climbing the steep front stoop, and finally pushing open the smooth glass door with a pale-green pane. I engage all my senses to do this. I then see myself walking through the front door and feeling happily overwhelmed by the yummy smells coming from the kitchen, my grandmother's Sunday sauce among them. I can hear the sound that the plastic on the furniture makes when someone sits on it. There's always a haze in the air from my uncle smoking his cigar, which I can smell, and I notice how the sunlight pushes through the smoke. As I walk through the room, I allow the images of my loved ones to be in the room with me. Sometimes the grandfather I never met is frying meatballs on the stove, and other times, my aunt is setting the table or turning on music. It's different each time.

Then, if the person I came to communicate with isn't there already, I call them in. I do this by finding a pair of places to sit, just like in the Creating a Psychic Contract meditation from chapter 3. I might choose the plastic-covered sofa or two wooden chairs at the kitchen table. (You can also do something similar with your spirit guides, but we'll bring in a loved one today.) When they show up — and they always do — I either let them start speaking or ask questions to prompt them.

Some people ask something specific, like "What do I need to understand about this situation?" or "What do you have to teach me?" I recommend staying away from yes-or-no questions — such as "Should I buy this property?" or "Is this relationship worth saving?" — because while Spirit may share an opinion that helps you make a decision, it's best to not go in with that expectation. Others go in looking for forgiveness — either to forgive or to be forgiven — which is nearly always offered. But more often than not, this tool simply elicits a deeply emotional, healing, validating experience. Just the meeting itself is enough.

Notice that this process doesn't avoid using your imagination — in fact, leaning into imaginative reality is a *requirement*. That's one of my favorite parts of Meeting Hours in Heaven, and it's one of the main reasons this practice works so well! Meeting Hours in Heaven is the best example I have of using your frame of reference to connect to Spirit. You are creating the scene — the sights, the sounds, the smells — with your imagination; you are accessing the memories of where you spent the most time with this person. Then, collectively, you and Spirit create this meditation together. It's actually quite easy, and that's why it's so powerful. You don't need to be a medium to do this, nor do you need to be all that far along the path of psychic development. Anyone can do it! It's totally DIY. (And it's also one of my personal favorite practices; I use it to connect with my loved ones all the time!)

As always, start with cleansing and grounding. Then read this meditation in full before beginning, or if you'd like, record it in your own voice and play it back. Add details as needed; this is *your* meditation!

Sit comfortably with a straight spine and your hands resting on your knees, palms up. Then pick a place that feels comfortable for you. If you're asking to meet a specific loved one, you may consider their home or the place where you spent the most time together. If you're open to meeting whichever loved one shows up, pick a place where your whole family used to gather.

Approach the place slowly and enter it. If there's a door or a gate, feel yourself opening it, walking through, and closing it behind you. Then start filling in the details of that place using your five senses. What smells and tastes do you experience? How does the temperature of the air feel on your skin? What sounds do you hear? Who else is there, and what are they doing? Allow your mind's eye to wander over all the details — if your location is inside, focus on the furniture, walls, ceiling, layout, knickknacks, and the like, and if it's outside, look to the plants, landscape, and sky. Then bring in two chairs, if there's not already a place for two to sit. These could be chairs that were actually in that space the last time you were there or chairs you saw somewhere else and remember clearly. Allow these to take shape, too, noticing all the details.

Breathing deeply, sit down in one of the chairs. Silently indicate to your Team that you are ready for your loved one to join you. Then just wait.

If it takes a minute, use that time to continue to go over the details of the space so it comes more alive.

Once your loved one joins you, you can do whatever you want. You can ask questions, hug, cry, confess — whatever calls you! If many loved ones come at once and you're overwhelmed, ask them to line up and take turns. These are your meeting hours, and you set the rules.

Take as long as you need to meet with your loved one(s). Notice how you feel as they offer you messages, which could come in the form of emotions, sensory input (sounds, smells, and so forth), or actual words. Be attentive to how it feels to experience this with the love and trust you have for your loved one. Be open to receiving what they have to share.

When you feel complete, thank your loved one for showing up.

Find your own way to say goodbye, knowing that you can always return to this place to meet again. Slowly allow the meeting space to fade away, return your consciousness to your body, and press your hands together to close the practice. If at all possible, journal about it right away so you can retain the benefits of Meeting Hours in Heaven.

Imagining What's Next

The more you practice getting comfortable with what's in your imagination, the more confident you'll become when delivering Spirit's messages. You're a conduit. All you have to do is receive the message and, if prompted, pass it along. Recognizing this is a good thing, because it takes the pressure off whether you're right or wrong. Frankly, it's not your job to say what *you* want to say but rather what *Spirit* wants you to say.

Whether you're harnessing your imagination for yourself or others, investing in Spirit's presence in this way is a necessary leap of faith. Because your imagination is already in place, you don't have to search for the source of the information you're conveying — it lives within you and always has, through your own frame of reference and Spirit's direction. You are already one with Spirit and already working with the guidance of your Team in all that you do. Once you believe that they're at the source of your words, thoughts, and actions when you lean on your instincts, you can stop worrying about whether it's all "real."

This confidence will accompany you throughout your journey of psychic development. And it will especially serve you as you start working with the next technique: finding your own set of tools for Spirit to use while communicating with you.

Chapter Five

TOOLS OF THE TRADE

Working with Crystals, Pendulums, and Cards

At some point in my childhood, I picked up a book on Tarot. I kept it in my room for years. I studied the pictures and read the commentary frequently, hoping it would unlock my secret gifts, looking for guidance on how to interpret the symbols and images on each card. The book's commentary was very straightforward — this card means this, that card means that — and though I didn't have the deck to accompany it, I would often ask a question and blindly select a page, first staring at the image and then reading to divine my answer.

I've forgotten most of what was in that book. It turned out that my fate was not to become a Tarot reader — or, at least, if that piece is coming, it hasn't yet unfolded. And though the book was fairly instructive in terms of the Tarot itself, it gave no information on the intuitive aspects of the process. I found myself wanting guidance on how, in a more general way, I could use the knowledge I gained about the Tarot as an extension of my own intuition.

Today, I have numerous spiritual card decks. I often draw from them for personal guidance. I used them in readings frequently in the past, when Spirit's messages were less clear to me. It's uncommon for me to bring them out publicly now, as I've learned more about my psychic gifts and how I am meant to contribute to the greater good. I am clear that my role is to receive messages from the Other Side. When cards aid in that effort, I use them, but most of the time, I don't.

I often think back to the process of figuring out how to work with that first Tarot book, though. As I experimented, I learned a lot about how to bring the more ethereal aspects of intuitive knowing here to this plane. Like crystals, pendulums, and oracle decks — all of which we will explore in the pages to come — Tarot is a serious spiritual tool that should be treated with respect. It's fine, perhaps even useful, to not always know what we're doing, as long as we don't use that learning period to experiment on a sitter. Whatever tool(s) we choose to work with, getting real, hands-on training is necessary if we want it to truly be spiritual lightwork. Yet for our own personal purposes, the *process* of learning to work with these tools can be quite helpful.

This chapter is therefore all about these tools and how you can start working with them. It attempts to fulfill what the Tarot book from my childhood didn't, offering a set of broader instructions about how psychic tools can work as an extension of intuition. First, I'll share what I know about some of the most commonly used tools. Then I'll explain how you can use tools — again, for your own guidance — to deepen the conversation with Spirit, creating a real back-and-forth dialogue through tangible means. By the end of the chapter, you'll be able to reach for the tools that call you and start gently, and respectfully, learning how they can help you develop your intuition and strengthen your connection with your Team.

A Range of Intuitive Tools

There are many types of tools that people use to develop intuition. Here, I'll provide a basic overview.

Crystals are quite high on this list. Many of my students have a strong affinity for crystals — sometimes even specific types of crystals — long before they come to work with me. Personally, I often find myself reaching for a crystal when I'm feeling out of sorts or I need some grounding. I rarely hang on to crystals for long, because I'm so often prompted to give them away; this makes it hard to really build a collection! But they can be very useful, especially in the short term.

Different types of crystals do different things. There's a whole area of study around what this or that crystal does — selenite cleans, for instance, while obsidian absorbs. If you're interested in that, or if you feel called to deepen your knowledge and add crystal work to your offerings for others, you will find a range of resources — such as books, workshops, and online and in-person classes — available to you.

There's a common saying about crystals: we don't choose the crystal; the crystal chooses us. For our purposes, whether you end up diving into the expansive world of crystals or not, this saying has a lot to offer. It can be very useful to experiment with feeling that pull toward a specific crystal and intuiting how the energy it holds might help. I'm not saying you'll be objectively *right* — perhaps you'll intuit something that is exactly the opposite of what someone else might say, which is precisely why you're only working on yourself at this stage. This exploration helps psychic development because the process of checking in with your intuitive knowing and divining what is best in each individual moment is instructive.

While I respect those who are well studied in crystals, I am not one of them myself. There's little rhyme or reason to the way I use crystals. I generally gravitate toward smaller crystals that I can hold. I sometimes put one on the table when I feel some negative energy around, with the intention that the negative energy be absorbed there instead of in my body. I'll put one in my pocket or my purse before going out, pulling it out casually in a public space and holding it in my hand. When I'm feeling particularly stimulated or like I've done too many readings, I'll keep a crystal in my pocket even when I'm at home. It doesn't happen frequently, but when I'm a little off or need extra energy, I always know I can grab a crystal to help me feel better.

Crystals can be very grounding, especially when there's a lot of psychic energy around or the vibration just feels busy. Many of my students have this experience, too; the right crystal at the right moment can stabilize our frequency, despite the other vibrations present, helping us to stay in our center as conduits of light.

Some crystals have been cut into a symmetrical shape and hung on a chain. This is called a pendulum. Pendulums are for divination. They're tools that help us answer questions. This tradition dates way back and is not limited to the crystal pendulums that are popular today. In my childhood, I witnessed older generations dangling a needle from thread in front of a pregnant belly to divine the sex of the baby within.

With a pendulum, different patterns of movement — such

as swinging front to back or side to side, or circling in one direction or another — are associated with different meanings. Many of my students have gained a lot from the process of sitting with the pendulum, because it gives them a clear experience of what their intuition feels like. For instance, we can ask the pendulum factual questions — usually, ones with a verifiable yes-or-no answer — to see how it swings. That way, we'll have a better sense of how it feels to land on a right answer, which will come in handy when we need to ask questions whose answers cannot be confirmed.

Oracle cards are also great for yes-or-no questions, though they work for open-ended questions as well. I love working with these decks! Sometimes, on those rare occasions I bring them into a reading, I don't even ask a question; I just pick a card for someone (or have them pick a card, if it's an in-person reading) and use it as a springboard for the rest of the reading. It provides a central theme, a way to organize the input coming my way. Near the end of this chapter, I have exact, step-by-step instructions for how to do this on your own.

My dear friend Gabrielle Bernstein's *Super Attractor* deck is one of my favorites — I just love the fresh, bright energy Gabby brings — and I also love the whimsical, multilayered artwork on Kyle Gray's cards. There are many great decks out there, so I encourage you to shop around. I highly recommend that if you're buying a deck, and *especially* if it's your first, you don't necessarily go for the most famous, the "best" according to someone else, or the one someone else once used on you. Instead, focus on the way the deck makes you feel. Which deck pulls you? Which catches your eye, your attention, your energy? *Follow that pull.* Consider the possibility that, like crystals, the decks are choosing you. As you work with identifying and responding to this intuitive pull, flexing it like a muscle, you'll get better at using it to pick an individual card from your deck, too.

Working with cards is a major avenue of study, and most decks come with a book or other material to help you sort through their meanings. Your intuition plays a large role as well. I've been told (though I never saw her do it) that my grandmother used to read playing cards like Tarot — she was operating on intuition alone. In fact, playing cards and Tarot come from the same cultural roots. It's absolutely fine if you don't know what you're doing and are relying entirely on intuitive hits, but be humble, and don't get overly serious about it — remember, this is exploratory, and the main goal is to figure out how your intuition signals you and how to respond.

Finally, we come back to the actual Tarot. I never did learn to use the Tarot properly. But if this is your calling, please go study it! My student Madeline has been working with Tarot for years, and she probably has loads to teach me at this point about the ins and outs of what each card means and how the different positions in a spread work together. At this point, Madeline is incredibly proficient at Tarot. In terms of accumulating knowledge, she's done her work. Yet I continue to instruct her about how to translate that through her own intuitive knowing, because that's well within my sphere of knowledge. She knows the literal interpretation of each card, as well as its placement, and I help her understand the message in between — the reason she's drawing the card, specifically, right now. This is purely psychic work, and it piggybacks on the more intellectual study Madeline does with her Tarot teacher. The Tarot signals something, and Madeline fleshes it out with her imagination, bringing herself into the work and expanding upon the Tarot as she provides readings for others as a psychic medium. If you're like Madeline, your guides will tell you, and if so, I highly encourage you to bolster your intuitive work with this tool by seeking out the more practical knowledge of qualified Tarot teachers.

That said, I still have more to offer on how and why you can work with these sorts of tools. Now that you have a basic understanding of some of the main tools out there, let's look at what they can offer as you develop your own psychic abilities.

When and Why to Use Tools

The psychic realms are ethereal. As human bridges between one world and another, we can easily feel like we lose contact with the earth. That's part of why we cleanse and ground regularly. (You *are* cleansing and grounding on a regular basis, aren't you? We'll return to this in chapter 7, but for now, if you still haven't cemented a cleansing and grounding practice or have been slacking lately, pick up the pace — it becomes increasingly important as your development progresses!) It's also the reason tools are so effective. In most cases, tools include physical objects, ones that exist right here on this plane. You can touch them, care for them, keep them on your altar. They're a physical representation of this work, and by treating them with respect, you're symbolically providing care for your psychic gifts.

They're also intellectual, meaning as we deepen our study of what calls us — taking a class on Tarot, for instance, or picking up a book on crystals — we give our brains something to *do*. In large part, psychic development is about taking that helpful, thinking mind and gently moving it out of the way so the intuition can get to work. But that's easier said than done! Sometimes distracting the mind, instead of just telling it to quiet down, is even more useful. This is why guided meditation and/or the repetition of a mantra is often easier than just sitting in silent meditation. We put our minds to work on something specific, freeing up space for the intuition to come into play. Collecting and synthesizing knowledge about the spiritual tools that call you works the same way.

It can be particularly beneficial to pull out a tool in the moments our minds are busy. When I first started reading for others, I'd often get nervous. My mind would come in and just start chatting away, often at the *exact* moment I really needed it to quiet down. Doubt would creep in, with all the negative self-talk that accompanies it — *Maybe you're not good enough, Maybe you can't do it, Maybe this is all absurd,* and so on — and I would seize up, petrified, not knowing where to even start. Cards and crystals were incredibly useful in these instances. Squeezing the crystal in my pocket for stability, I would suggest that the sitter pick a card. As they shuffled the deck, the vibration would shift, and we would enter a new space together. Then, letting my eyes rest on the card, I would allow the imagery to instruct my imagination, relaxing the "doing" part just enough that Spirit could step in to direct the show. Sometimes the sitter would tell me their question; other times they wouldn't. The card would allow me to answer it regardless by giving me a framework, a springboard from which to launch a connection. This was enormously helpful in my early years as a working psychic medium.

Tools can also help when we're overwhelmed by input and have *too much* to say. They're tangible, physical, present — qualities that come in handy when our clairs are saturated with information. Sometimes there's plenty of imagery, but we're not able to organize it. It seems contradictory, or it's clouded by heavy emotions like fear, anxiety, and grief. We need clarity and direction, and tools can provide them.

As we enter into this intuitive study, it's important to understand that no matter what tool we use to communicate with

Spirit, our guides are always in charge. If we need a tool to help us focus, they'll find a way to speak through it, no problem. The inspiration to use a tool almost always comes from them in the first place. They want to give us the clarity we're looking for, so they plant the idea in our mind via one of the clairs to facilitate the process.

Now that you understand when and why to use tools, let's consider how you can go about exploring your relationship to them.

How to Use Tools

When working with tools, there are two important things to keep in mind: respect your tools and don't attach to them.

We'll start with tool care and hygiene. As objects that transmit psychic energy, tools need to be treated with respect. They are spiritual items, objects devoted to honoring and communicating with Spirit — like us, they are conduits that bring psychic energy to this plane. That means they're energetically sensitive. They pick up the vibrations of the environment and people around them. It's nice to give them their own place in your house, perhaps even stored in a box, in a case, or wrapped in a nice piece of cloth. It's best if they can be undisturbed, because they need special attention when someone else's energy passes through them.

Anytime anyone besides you touches any of your tools for any reason, clean them energetically. And unless there's a strong reason for someone to do so — say, they're going to pick a card, or you feel guided to hand them a crystal to hold during the reading — it's generally better if you handle your own accoutrements. There's nothing wrong with others touching them, but it requires cleanup afterward to keep the energies separate and clear.

Tools also need to be cleansed when, despite our attempts to avoid it, a little bit of negative energy slips through. Grounding ourselves and regularly affirming our intention that our spiritual work always serves the highest good of all involved are our best ways to keep negative energy from touching our tools, but sometimes it happens — we're really upset, or we've just had a long and intense cry, or maybe we're even connecting with Spirit because we're really angry at someone and we want comfort to help us process it. We show up with the best energy we have, and afterward, we can clean our tools.

Cleansing tools is a simple process. It's a ritual that can be done in many ways; however your guides lead you to do it is fine, as long as you're clear on your intention to purify and return the tool to its original state so it can continue to transmit light. I love sage, so I most often smudge things. With cards, this is usually the easiest way. I've seen other people use holy water on their crystals or even put them out in the light of the full moon. (Some minerals don't mix well with water, so be sure to check first.) Maria, one of my psychic friends, works with crystals a lot, and she loves to put them out in the moonlight. She does a small ritual around this every month, barefoot in her backyard with a sound bowl. I love that! If you feel called to go to such lengths, follow the pull, and if you don't, just set your intention and light your sage. *How* you cleanse is far less important than *whether* you do it; the takeaway here is that if you want your tools to work well, you need to clean them regularly.

Pull your guides in on this — they can help. Ask them to help you clean your tools and to keep them clean between uses. If you want, you can place your tools near selenite, sage, holy water, or any other cleansing element, and set the intention that they will naturally be kept clean by proximity. This is how my friend Jane does it — no effort required! Together with your guides, you'll find the best way for you.

Your guides can also help out with this next part: the part about not attaching to your tools. As I wrote at the beginning of the chapter, I frequently give crystals away. There are several I have had for many years, but the vast majority pass through my hands within months, sometimes even weeks! That doesn't mean you have to give everything away — some Tarot readers work with the same deck for decades, and I doubt anyone would *want* to work with someone else's used deck, unlike crystals that have changed hands. But it *does* mean that attachment doesn't serve anyone when tools are involved. If you lose a beloved crystal or forget to bring your deck to a friend's house one night, let it go, knowing that your Team is taking care of you and everything is just as it should be. If your best attempt to care for your tools well is thwarted — if your puppy eats your oracle cards or a crystal breaks — forgive yourself and do better next time, trusting that all is well. If you *always* use one tool and one day find yourself reaching for another, follow that urge. The thinking mind attaches, but intuition is always fluid.

This form of nonattachment isn't just literal; it's also a philosophy. It means approaching tools with accountability, being ready to expand on them with your own frame of reference and interpret them your own way, without getting your ego involved in whether or not you're *right*; it means being ready, again and again, to go back to the basics and learn more. As a result, you may work with a tool for years, consistently growing your skill set. You may also work with a tool for some time before plateauing, or setting it down for a while, only to pick it up again when your guides signal it's time. Though, as I've mentioned, I used to bring oracle cards out a lot in readings, nowadays I don't very often. Usually, they stay on my book-shelf, and I use them for myself. Maybe someday I will be guided to do something different, and I'm open to that!

Staying unattached requires humility. It calls for us to recognize that our guides are always in charge and we're just following directions. That means when we get the sudden in-spiration to carry a crystal in our pocket, pull a card on our way out the door, or put a spiritual image on our bedside table, we trust that it's our guides telling us this tool can be helpful, and we don't even need to know the reason — we just act. If we're drawn to a certain tool for a while, to develop a specific skill set and even offer it to others, we do that, too. Our guides are al-ways working to make sure we are grounded and protected and have the best tools available to spread our spiritual lightwork through the world. They're trying to take care of us — and we have to let them!

Kristen, a student I have worked with for many years, used oracle cards regularly when she began giving psychic readings. She initially picked them up to help ground her readings, and over time she developed a real skill at interpreting what they meant for her sitters. Eventually, her guides prompted her to move on from the cards, suggesting that she had arrived at a state of psychic development where she could deliver more specific and thoughtful messages without them. Had she been attached, this message would have been hard to receive, but fortunately, Kristen understood that Spirit would never lead her astray. She did one reading without the cards, then another, then another. At first, she was nervous, but she quickly learned that her Team had her back; she *was* ready to read without the cards, and her sitters all benefited from her bravery.

The same is true with any methodology, beyond just the physical tools available to us. Like Kristen, I drifted away from oracle cards over time. For many years, I would write on a notepad during most readings — or, better put, I would scribble wildly on it, letting Spirit direct my pen. Automatic writing provided focus for me. I could look down and see a word repeated three times, signaling it referred to a very important message Spirit wanted me to deliver. One day, I forgot my notebook. I pushed through the reading, knowing my guides would not have let me do that if it weren't intentional. Then it happened again, and again. Eventually, I stopped automatic writing during readings completely. As it turned out, it was just in time; a few months later, I started giving large-group readings, an environment in which I simply couldn't automatic-write, even if I'd had the desire. I realized then that my guides had been preparing me for that moment all along.

The final way attachment can show up is through the overuse of tools or even the more general overuse of our gift. This is a mash-up between a boundary issue and an ego issue. Sometimes we get really excited, especially when we're new to this work or new gifts are emerging, and want to read everyone and everything. Or we just want to read ourselves and our own lives, peppering our deck or our pendulum with questions. We get hopped up on psychic energy like a kid with a sugar rush. If we aren't keeping ourselves balanced and regularly checking in with our energy reserves, we can start to become too reliant on tools, using them like a crutch. This isn't healthy. Everyone has their own experience of it — the difference between using a tool and abusing it is quite subtle, and it looks different for different people — but keep this in your consciousness when you go to work with tools.

Throughout your work with spiritual tools, let it be your own journey, with your guides leading the way. The following practice will help get you started.

PRACTICE

··∙)∘(⸱···

Exploring Oracle Cards

Oracle cards can help us access our own intuitive knowledge as well as messages from the Other Side. Many people keep a deck on their altar. Some draw a card every morning to provide guidance for the day. Others consult their deck when they have a specific question to ask or an issue that they would like to understand better.

While there's no "right" way to care for oracle cards, there is a consensus that the way we take care of them matters. We're accountable for handling them carefully, keeping them where they will not be disturbed, regularly clearing them of outside energy, and generally tending to their well-being. This means different things to different people, so let your guides indicate what it means for you.

When we work with cards, it's important that we trust the answers we receive. Though we may not be clear on the interpretation, because that part is often quite nuanced, we trust in the fact that we have, indeed, received the right card! Many people have had the experience of rejecting the card they pulled, putting it back in the deck, shuffling, and drawing another — only to find that it's the same card again. Other times, a card will just pop out of the deck, or we'll try to draw one and two or three will come instead. Trust that this is Spirit, every time, utilizing the tool along with you and offering up the exact card(s) you need. This is always true, whether the meaning is immediately obvious or you have no idea how to interpret the message.

To do this exercise, you'll need a spiritual deck (angel cards, oracle cards, or Tarot cards, though we won't be creating a Tarot spread), and you may want a journal and a pen.

Take a minute to ground yourself before pulling out your deck. Get present first. This doesn't have to be a big ceremony; it can even be just a few conscious breaths. If your cards need energetic cleansing with sage or anything else, go for it, and if you haven't cleansed or grounded your energy lately, do so now. These aren't things you have to do every time you use oracle cards — in a pinch, you can definitely pull a card quickly, car keys in hand, on your way out the door. But if you're going to take the time to sit down and really question your cards, give them the respect of showing up completely. You are 100 percent accountable for determining what that means for you — and your Team can always help out.

Next, hold the cards loosely in one hand and use the other to shuffle them, letting them be infused with your energy as you do. (If and when you feel the call to read for others, you'll have the sitter shuffle the cards, too, and you'll smudge or otherwise cleanse the deck after the reading is finished.) I like to infuse my energy into the cards by centering myself and allowing my mind to relax to the point of going almost blank momentarily, and if I have a question, I let it emerge from that expanse of space. Sometimes I know what question I will ask beforehand; sometimes I don't, but one pops up and I roll with it; sometimes I don't ask a question at all. Today, we'll use a series of questions. Go big, go small; it doesn't matter. Just let the questions pop into your head.

Consider using open-ended questions, like:

- *What should I do in ___ situation?*
- *How can I better understand my relationship with ___?*
- *What do I need to know or learn to make a decision regarding ___ [a career path, romance, friendship, financial endeavor, etc.]?*
- *What would help me grow spiritually?*
- *What do my guides want to tell me?*
- *Loved one, what would you have me know in this moment?*
- *What am I not seeing?*

Depending on the deck you have, it may also be possible to ask yes-or-no questions, like:

- *Should I quit my job?*
- *Is this relationship ready to go deeper?*

- *Should I make this specific [housing, business, or financial] decision?*

Holding the deck, ask your first question. Then set it down on the floor or a table in front of you. Holding your question in your consciousness, cut the deck and draw your card.

Here, some people like to put the card facedown and breathe for a moment before revealing what's on the reverse, while others turn the card over right away. This is the DIY part: I trust that whatever specific mini-ritual you're guided to do is the right one. Experiment with it! See what feels good for you.

As you study the card, first let your imagination wander a bit. Read any words on the card and let your eyes roam over the details of the imagery it contains. Does it remind you of anything? Does it bring up an emotional response? Does it trigger anything within your frame of reference? Use the five-second rule and take the first answers you receive seriously, even if they feel random or absurd. Make a mental note of them or, if you like, jot them down in your journal.

Then do two minutes of research. If there's a book or booklet that accompanies your deck, read the information there, or search the internet briefly. The card's title is a good place to start, but follow your intuition as you research. Sometimes a certain plant or animal will be pictured on a card, and that may have some meaning. Sometimes the colors, shapes, or themes will bring something up for you.

Sit for a moment with whatever information you gathered, and then consider this in connection to what you intuited a few minutes ago. Let the two intertwine, and then let your imagination begin to assign meaning to their combined form. Again, do this quickly — trust the first things that come. Spirit often makes it through in those first five seconds.

You may find that the card has obvious meaning to you right away. Even when this isn't the case with my students, they often eventually reveal that they think it *might* mean something, *maybe* — if you have even an inkling like that, go with it. If images,

particularly symbolic ones, come into your mind's eye, pay attention. Whatever you make or "might" make of the card, honor that
meaning. Breathe into it and, if you like, write it down.

Then return the card to the deck. Shuffle again as you ask your
next question, and repeat. Ask as many questions as you'd like before thanking the cards, shuffling them a bit to release the process,
and respectfully putting them away.

Dedicating Our Tools to the Greatest Good

Whenever we work with a tool, the most important truth to
hold is that we're using this item for the greatest good. We put
our ego aside and become a conduit of light, understanding
that *we* are not the ones providing these answers or generating
this energy, nor does the tool itself hold that sort of power. The
wisdom and strength emanating from the tool comes directly
from Spirit. We have to call that higher power to be with us,
and we have to keep our tools protected and cared for, because
that's the only way that process can take place.

How we do those things is up to each one of us. I am a
firm believer that there are many "right" ways, and many of the
best intuitives I teach also work with other teachers for specific
spiritual and intuitive disciplines. I trust their Teams to guide
them, as I trust yours to guide you.

We're also accountable for our own interpretation. To truly
be conduits for Spirit, we have to remove our own ideas and
opinions from the interpretation while searching for the most
positive option available. This is what it takes to deliver useful
information, effectively transmitting spiritual wisdom from
one plane to another.

Chapter Six

MASTER YOUR DELIVERY

Learning the Customer Service of Spirituality

Once we are comfortable receiving information from Spirit, it's time to learn how to deliver careful and respectful messages that resonate. Delivery covers all aspects of translating psychic input into a clear, direct message. It involves how we understand the messages we receive and how we ascribe meaning to them. It also involves what we do with that meaning as we attempt to accurately and respectfully communicate what we receive from Spirit to others.

Delivery is one of the most crucial parts of this work. In this chapter, we'll look at delivery from a few different angles. First, you'll learn to start interpreting the input you receive. This takes the ideas we explored in chapter 4 to the next level, putting everything you have learned about the unique way Spirit communicates with you into practice. Then we'll return to this idea of positivity, and I'll explain exactly how to find the positive version of any message you receive. Finally, we'll consider delivering messages with care, concern, and compassion, which is essential whether you're reading formally or channeling advice.

It's up to us as developing psychics to represent Spirit as best we can, whether we're channeling for ourselves or for others. Whether we're giving past-life readings, advising about the future, downloading messages from light beings here to guide us, or transmitting messages from loved ones on the Other Side, accurate and effective delivery is a massive part of the task.

The Art of Interpretation

Interpretation, or making sense of the input we receive from Spirit, is all about giving symbolic meaning to specific aspects of our unique frame of reference. We first looked at symbols in chapter 4. As we begin to catalog the different meanings of the symbols we receive, a certain automatic function comes into ascribing meaning. This is part of the reason I encourage working with the five-second rule. It trains us to just grab onto the first idea that pops up and roll with it, without pulling the thinking (and often doubting) mind on board to make a mess of everything.

What is initially a five-second response becomes quicker over time. We repeat the action, letting our intuition free-associate without judgment, until it happens in two seconds, then one, then half a second. When that action is overlaid with a set of symbols that is unique to us, we can just free-associate our way through a psychic reading — and because we're practiced at tapping into the psychic realm, the reading is *accurate*. It becomes surprisingly simple.

Despite our best efforts to be conduits, we are naturally a part of the interpretation. We strive to get out of the way, but since the information is coming *through* us, it's also coming through our frame of reference. That means if we make one wrong assumption, our free association can lead us on a wild-goose chase.

Lindsay, who trained with me for a couple of years, provides an example. She was battling a variety of medical issues, and because her mind was already focused on her own health, she often misinterpreted psychic messages about other people's health. Though the information she received was accurate, she was unconsciously inserting her own concerns into the interpretation. "Ooh! Your dad's heart is not looking good," Lindsay once announced ominously to another student during an exercise. The other student looked at me, panicked and desperate, for confirmation. I suspected this was not the correct interpretation, so I asked Lindsay to back it up a bit. She explained that she had seen a man in his sixties walking briskly on the beach and, being acutely aware of cardiovascular health herself, had assumed he was caring for his heart. From there, I saw that Lindsay had jumped into her own fear of cardiac arrest. She'd followed the five-second rule, but her assumption had confused the interpretation. We talked about it a little bit more, and Lindsay was able to back off her assumption and see the rest of the scene: a dog running after a Frisbee, and a child building a sandcastle. As it turned out, she was describing the other student's recent family vacation! From there, Lindsay was able to channel the rest of the message — and it had nothing to do with cardiac health.

This example shows us that interpretation can be quite

tricky. In chapter 4, we considered how we inherently must use our own imagination and frame of reference to channel Spirit. We must open ourselves to believe that our own experiences are accurately conveying meaning to us. Yet at a certain point in our psychic development, when we really drill down into delivery, we learn to sustain that openness — to have confidence without becoming rigid in our thinking. In truth, the "heart issues" interpretation was one of perhaps dozens that flipped through Lindsay's mind in that moment; she got off track when she seized on it, brought her own fears into the mix, and decided it was true.

One thing that can help prevent this from happening is to focus on the positive. Again and again, we're accountable for looking for the most affirming interpretation available — the one that inspires confident action, whether it's our own Team guiding our actions or another person's guide or loved one hoping to communicate through us. Either way, something like Lindsay's original message — the one that threw her classmate into a panic, thinking her father was about to have a heart attack — isn't particularly helpful, which is part of how I intuitively knew she wasn't interpreting it correctly. Sometimes we have to pause for a moment, but the positive information is always there, waiting for us to find it.

It's Always Positive

There's nearly always a way to find the positive in a message, even when our initial response is to see what we receive in a negative light.

In my experience, Spirit never shows up to say, "Hey, look at all this terrible stuff that happened," and leave it at that. The purpose of showing us dark things is that in doing so, Spirit indicates exactly where the light needs to go. Our Team is trying to offer guidance, and to help us make sense of that guidance, they're showing us the precise context in which it will be most useful.

Since it's my role to pass on messages from loved ones, I often encounter people in deep and raw grief. Grief is painful, yet it's not an inherently bad thing; it comes straight from Spirit, and it serves a purpose. And since I'm empathic, I allow myself to feel the grief of others to a small degree — I let it in, just a little — because I always want to come from a space of compassion. Then, to make sure I can be of the greatest service, I hold a firm boundary, leaving the majority of the grief outside my energy field. I may still continue to witness the grief the other person is feeling, though, especially if Spirit wants me to see it. This means I sometimes pick up on heavy images and sensations of grief, even though I don't embody them emotionally myself.

When I see this repeatedly, it means the grief has become all-consuming. Spirit is suggesting that while grief itself is healthy and should not be bypassed, we also don't need to feed it, just like we don't feed fear, and loved ones in Spirit want me to convey this message to the grieving sitter in front of me. I've been asked to pass on a similar message on numerous occasions. Loved ones often want to address the grief first and foremost because it's such a source of pain for those left on Earth.

This is a delicate situation. As the medium, I'm accountable for delivering a loved one's message in a positive light. I therefore don't want to just blurt out, "Listen, I know this is rough, but you're going to need to just get over it; your loved one doesn't want you to hang on to them, OK?" Can you imagine?! This would be entirely unkind, and it certainly wouldn't land in any constructive way with the sitter. Instead, I could phrase it as "Your loved one sees and feels how you are grieving and wants you to learn to live with your grief— allow it to arise when it needs to, but don't let it take over your life. Can you see ways in which you could keep living your life, despite your grief? This is the way your loved one longs to see you." Do you hear the difference in tone? There's also a difference in the action requested — instead of "stop doing this," it becomes "start doing that." This makes it much more accessible and practical for the one receiving the message.

The same is true when we're channeling for ourselves. Often, the slip into negative interpretation doesn't happen in the psychic's communication with the sitter but rather in the way the psychic makes sense of the input they receive. When I have a nightmare, for instance, I interpret it to be a message from Spirit. I could focus on the scary part, the fact that the message was delivered in a fear-inducing package, and think Spirit was sending me darkness; if that happened, I wouldn't have any reason to investigate the dream further, because it's not within my boundaries to deal in dark energy. Or I could focus on the intensity, the fact that the message was delivered in a way that was absolutely 100 percent guaranteed to get my attention. This positive interpretation makes it possible to derive wisdom and guidance from the dream, seeing the greater meaning behind the themes that appeared in my own subconscious.

With even the darkest of messages we can ask ourselves, *What else could this mean?* That option is infinitely available to us, especially when we come to understand the role it plays in accurate interpretation. Again, this isn't about denial; it's about getting the most we can out of the input Spirit gives us. We can do this through contemplation or automatic writing, either spontaneously in the moment or as part of a regular practice. If we have time, we can go to our temple in meditation and ask our guides directly: "With great respect, I don't get this. Why did you send me that stuff? What are you trying to show me? What do I need to understand better?" We can sit with the question, again and again: *What is the most positive translation available for this set of images or ideas?*

Often, these positive messages can be found in the little stuff — the small details that surround a dark or heavy message. In many years of doing this, I have consistently observed that the most meaningful things I communicate to a sitter are often the ones that seem least significant to me. I'll remind a bereaved husband of the day he and his wife had a picnic by the lake early in their courtship, or a devastated daughter of her mom's hug to welcome her home at six years old, after she announced that she was running away, furiously packing her clothes and toys into the front basket of her bike. I'll share laughter and joy with them as Spirit recalls these poignant memories. Spirit most often just wants to share love with those of us who are still living — many times, I've been asked to tell the sitter to "remember me laughing." Whenever I find myself trying to "make" the reading into something, I back off and ask for these small details.

It is crucial that we practice finding the positive interpretation before we start sharing what we intuit with others. That starts with believing, at the deepest level, that Spirit only ever sends us darkness to show us the light.

Sharing What We Intuit with Others

Once we find the positive interpretation of the information we receive, we can consider whether it's meant to be passed along. If it is, we must be sure to deliver it with the 3 Cs: *care, concern,* and *compassion*. We do this by considering all the options for how the message we send might be received: *What will the sitter do with this information? Is it even wanted? Could it be hurtful, scary, or shocking? How might hearing what Spirit has to say comfort, help, or reassure the person sitting in front of me right now?*

Whether we're formally channeling or just counseling a friend, it's an honor to provide guidance and advice to others. It's also an enormous responsibility. Anytime we're in the position of guiding another person through uncertainty or pain, we have an opportunity to help or hurt. We intend to help, and the way we put this intention into action matters. Everyone involved must therefore be treated with the utmost respect. Ultimately, we walk the psychic path to be of service to Spirit; the 3 Cs keep us connected to that fact.

Consider what it takes to give good advice as a friend. We're most supportive and available to each other when we first show up with the 3 Cs. Then, if feedback is requested, we can bring the more positive, open-ended aspects of our opinions into the mix ("It sounds like that relationship isn't serving you the way it used to") and leave the stronger, harder opinions out ("I never did like Joe — you should definitely break up with him"). In truth, I run a psychic reading the very same way — I rarely tell anyone exactly what to do, because my guides rarely ask me to. This leads to a more empowering reading because it allows the sitter to receive functional guidance that they can choose to either follow or not.

The same principle applies to channeled advice outside of a reading. Channeled advice is a fantastic way to deliver information from the psychic realm. For many psychics, myself included, there comes a moment of reckoning when we realize exactly how much of our advice has been channeled all along. We can present channeled information as advice, too, particularly when it's the best way for the other person to hear it. It's often not necessary to tell someone, "Your grandmother told me you should look into this" — especially if they didn't ask. It may be much more helpful to just mention the idea in conversation.

Just like in a traditional psychic reading, when we offer channeled advice we often just know what we're saying is true. Yet we're accountable for not demanding that the person receiving our advice do what we say. I mention this because frequently we feel quite adamant about channeled information. We're passionate, certain, unshakable. Yet part of following the 3 Cs requires addressing and softening our approach, even when there's a psychic aspect to the advice we're offering.

One of my students, Mina, provides the perfect example. While she was taking classes with me, her husband lost his mother to addiction. Mina had a vision wherein her mother-in-law came and explained what happened, weeping as she showed Mina her state of desperation in the weeks leading up to her death. She urgently wanted her son, Mina's husband, to know how she felt. Yet he was skeptical of his wife's psychic connection, and Mina was worried he would reject her vision.

When Mina brought this situation up to me, I encouraged her to look for the most positive information to share with her grieving husband. Addiction is an incredibly sensitive topic, especially for bereaved family members. She focused in on the complex emotional experience her mother-in-law had expressed: from the depth of her addiction to the strength of her love for so many people, like her son. Mina saw that her mission was to help her husband explore these feelings and connect more deeply to his mother's experience, and she realized that she didn't have to explain the vision to make that happen. In the end, Mina opted not to tell him about the vision or recount the painful images she had seen — this would not have followed the 3 Cs. Instead, she opened a deep conversation, listening and holding space as her husband found a connection with his mother's emotional state. Sure enough, this action achieved Spirit's objective.

Mina's story is important because it demonstrates that there are many ways to deliver psychic information. That's good news, because it's not appropriate to just walk up to someone in the grocery store and start channeling her grandfather — nor is it appropriate to channel the grandfather of your best friend in your very own kitchen if that friend did not ask you to do so. The 3 Cs apply to everything we share as well as everything we don't.

I have a strong personal boundary around only reading people who request it. This doesn't stop anyone from getting through, though — those in Spirit know what they're doing! For example, there was once a terrible accident in which a man from my town died. I'll call him Jim. I had many mutual contacts with Jim's wife, and as the shock of the event rippled out through our community, several friends asked me to do a reading for her. Though I had met her a few times, I didn't know her well. I knew it was absolutely inappropriate to offer her a reading if she hadn't requested one. But sure enough, Jim started coming to me in Spirit with information for his wife. He knew she was shocked by his sudden departure. I told Jim I couldn't read for his wife unless she approached me and requested it.

Jim took this on as his personal mission. Shortly thereafter, I was doing a reading for a different woman, unrelated to the couple. I was surprised to feel Jim's energy there. "Not now," I intoned. "You don't even know this woman." He persisted, going to great lengths to get through to me — like Patrick Swayze's character did to Whoopi Goldberg's character in *Ghost*. He just wouldn't let it go! Finally, I said aloud, "Listen, I know this is wild, but there's this guy here, Jim, who just died recently. I don't think you know him, but he wants me to tell you something." The sitter gasped: she *did* know Jim and his wife — quite well, in fact! In the coming weeks this happened twice more in both individual and group readings, and Jim popped up at a couple of social events, too. Jim was like a party crasher — he didn't care that he wasn't invited, because he just wanted to join in on the fun! And he was highly motivated to get through to his wife in any way he could.

It worked; eventually, his wife called me. "People keep telling me I have to work with you," she said. "My husband is busting into *their* psychic readings to get through to me, though I guess I'm not surprised!" As it turned out, the humorous messages and persistence Jim displayed in Spirit lined up perfectly with the man she had fallen in love with so many years before, and she was delighted that he was relatively unchanged. It brought her enormous comfort to realize that her husband was, in fact, OK — even though he was no longer alive. This was only possible because Jim's wife was ready to receive his messages. I focused on her needs, treating her with care, concern, and compassion every step of the way, and Jim saw to the rest.

The 3 Cs will help you kindly deliver the messages you receive. For you to do so successfully, they must first be clear. The practice that comes next will help you find a clear, positive interpretation of the messages you receive, whether they're intended for you or others.

PRACTICE

···)∘⋲···

Clarifying the Messages You Receive

No matter what we receive from Spirit, we are accountable for finding a positive way to interpret it. To translate something negatively doesn't serve us or anyone else. It's a waste of our gifts.

Spirit sends messages that can serve — exclusively. That's

always the aim. This exercise is all about aligning you to Spirit's greater mission.

When we receive information that initially appears negative, our first move is to pause. Then we check our ego and reaffirm that we are delivering messages for the greater good of all concerned. Once we've done that, we set to work finding the positive interpretation within the message.

This requires us to relax our gaze a bit. We have to know the voice of our own fear and doubt well so it doesn't take over our thinking. We're called to use our imagination and frame of reference while also broadening it beyond our own limited thinking — a delicate task, to be sure. It takes practice, but it's worth it.

For this practice you'll need a journal and a pen. Draw three columns on a page, and start by writing down an unclear message — a dream, a vision, a repetitive image, a piece of automatic writing, or any other input from Spirit that feels negative or difficult to translate — in the left column.

List your first responses to this message in the middle column. Any automatic, knee-jerk responses go here.

Then look for the positive interpretation. Ask yourself, *Why would I see that? What is Spirit trying to say? What could I do with that information?* List possible answers in the right column.

UNCLEAR MESSAGE	FIRST RESPONSE	POSSIBLE POSITIVE INTERPRETATION
Dream: I'm back in school, at my desk, and there is an exam. I haven't studied and am entirely unprepared. In fact, I don't even know what the test is about!	*Panic!* I'm unprepared for my life. I'm going to fail at everything.	I'm still learning and need to prepare for a big lesson coming my way. What is the subject I'm not facing?

Vision: I see myself suddenly pregnant and about to give birth.	I'm literally pregnant and about to give birth?! Now?! What terrible timing!	New beginnings! Something creative is being born from me.
Repetitive image: I keep seeing or noticing the numbers "911."	Emergency! Catastrophe! Something is about to go wrong!	This is an urgent call to action. What needs attention in my life?

Hang on to this page and add a new row anytime you receive an unclear or negative message. As you do, you'll start to see patterns around what triggers you. Like Lindsay, who was highly focused on health, you'll begin to see your own shadow in the negative interpretations that arise. There's no need to judge yourself or feel bad about what you see; you're only human! But collecting this information is a great way to keep yourself in check so your delivery can make the biggest impact. Knowing your own patterns is essential to helping you stay connected to positivity in the future.

Delivering Responsibly

In many ways, delivery is where the real work begins. We're accountable to the light. We're responsible for what we do with the input we receive — how we give it meaning and how we put that meaning into action, which sometimes includes conveying messages to others.

This requires trust. At a certain point in our journey of psychic development, we begin to trust Spirit completely. We learn to honor the incredible gifts we have been given and to celebrate them by tending them well. Spiritual connection becomes the underpinning of every aspect of our lives, because we know we're not alone, and we're in healthy dialogue with

those who guide us. Then the work becomes something new —
it's no longer about attaining something at the end of the
journey but instead about keeping ourselves balanced along
the way.

Chapter Seven

DON'T YOU DABBLE!

Creating and Sustaining a Spiritual Practice

There comes a time in every psychic's life when things get serious.

Don't get me wrong — it can still be fun. In fact, a light-hearted attitude is required! Humor, joy, and laughter are always welcome.

Yet at a certain point, that spontaneous, joyful experience needs strong grounding for us to really flourish. The spiritual steps we take become dependent on our ability to take our role seriously. At a certain point, not doing so becomes irresponsible. Yes, we are playful, but no, we are not playing around. We're simply no longer able to dabble in it.

Each one of us makes this shift at a different point in

time. For some, it's in response to a life crisis. For others, it's when they start hearing the call to read for other people. Still others have crossed this threshold even before they begin working on their psychic development. Many of us learn the hard way not to dabble in psychic development when it becomes exceedingly uncomfortable to *not* make some sort of regular commitment to our spiritual practice. Even though it takes some doing, we recognize that our efforts are swiftly rewarded.

This book's seventh technique outlines exactly what adopting a regular spiritual practice looks like and what it means for you as a developing psychic medium. Like I do with everything in these pages, I'll point you in the right direction, and it will be up to you to adapt it to fit your needs. I'll lead you through creating your own connection with your practice, focusing primarily on consistency.

First, we'll look at what happens when we dabble in the psychic realms and why doing so can be harmful. Then I'll explain how even the busiest and/or least disciplined person can, in fact, create a habit of checking in with their guides and honoring Spirit. We'll consider why *remembering* to do this is almost as important as the action itself, understanding the benefits to the rest of your life that this regular practice can offer. At the end of the chapter, you'll have a chance to create your own spiritual schedule for the upcoming week, a practice many of my students have found useful as they cross the threshold into making a habit of spiritual connection.

In many ways, this chapter marks a turning point. It's an essential shift in the way we approach psychic development. And it's also when we start to experience the deepest, most calming and present form of support we've ever known.

Dabbling Makes Drama

As I shared in the preface, I spent many years of my life without a regular practice. I had it stashed somewhere in the back of my mind that I could one day become an accomplished psychic, as John Edward had foretold to my mother. I wasn't attached to this vision, though — it seemed like one of many possibilities, and not necessarily the one I was most focused on manifesting into reality. I worked in retail sales before stepping back to be with my kids, and on the tail end of those long and lovely years at home, I became active in their school.

I was also baptized Catholic and went on to take Communion and receive the rite of confirmation. I loved the years I spent going to church every Sunday. It gave me a framework to hold many of the spiritual beliefs I had always had and offered a set of rituals to match. The process I went through with Catholicism as an adult formed much of my understanding around the importance of spiritual practice. I am still a Catholic, and I find great meaning in the practices of the church. But over time I started reaching for some of the techniques that had interested me as a child, like cards and meditation, and incorporating them into my spiritual practice as well. I began to ask for this guidance more often. Repetition became habit.

The crucial shift occurred when *not* practicing began to tug at me. I started to develop a sense when things were off — not something fear based or superstitious but a nagging feeling that I needed to recenter myself and connect with the guidance that is always there, available and waiting. It was as if the universe were asking me to check in. Instead of turning to prayer just when things were especially tough, I started communicating with my Team consistently in small ways throughout my day.

We have the opportunity to create a wonderful relationship with Spirit in all its forms, as well as with ourselves through trusting our own intuition, but to get the benefits of that relationship we have to nourish it. We have to pay attention to it.

The best way to develop most new skills is to acquire a basic education and then practice, practice, practice. It's like building a spiritual muscle. As with any other muscle, when we don't use it, it will grow weak. We're accountable for exercising it day by day. If we do, we can pretty much guarantee that the muscle will grow stronger. If we don't, we can pretty much guarantee that the muscle will atrophy.

Just like with a physical exercise practice, it's OK to have a cheat day. We don't need to beat ourselves up over things like that. But if we cheat *too* much — if we allow ourselves to lose our drive and become inconsistent — we can't wonder why we don't see results. Our relationship with our guides has everything to do with our participation and nothing to do with theirs. They're always there, just waiting for us to connect; we are the ones who need to condition our spiritual muscles to meet them. When we don't, it just doesn't work.

Dabbling feeds doubt, and doubt makes drama. When we're inconsistent, we often find ourselves wondering why our attempts at psychic connection are ineffective. We ask what's wrong with us and suspect that our future attempts will be similarly unfruitful. When we dabble, it's easy for us to regress to mistrust. Perceiving Spirit feels more difficult than it has in the past, and we're often shaky on how to translate the messages we receive. The reason for this is simple: we're simply out of practice. Because so much of psychic and intuitive knowing is based on confidence, however, it can be particularly detrimental.

Our response to our own inconsistency can cause further

difficulty, increasing doubt even more. Maybe we throw ourselves into a long, in-depth guided meditation or spend the whole morning automatic-writing in response. Perhaps we buy another book or sign up for another workshop. We're desperate to make the connection again. While these isolated efforts count for something, and while meditations, automatic writing, books, and workshops are definitely recommended for everyone's long-term psychic development, they often don't address our issue in the short term. The reason for this is that the most important factor is actually showing up consistently. If we walk away from our meditation or a workshop having achieved the connection we were seeking, we may feel inspired — but if we don't, we feel let down. Our efforts serve to spiral us away from psychic development, instead of bringing us closer to it.

Consistency is what brings us back to our center. This commitment doesn't have to be big or even time-consuming. It doesn't have to overtake our life; it just has to be regular and frequent. It's a slight shift in many ways and a massive spiritual lifestyle change in others. This is the moment when we move beyond fulfilling our curiosity or exploring a hobby; we're making a commitment to ourselves, to our souls. It's therefore up to each of us to figure out what consistency in spiritual practice means in our own context.

Your Schedule, Your Way

Once we commit to a regular spiritual practice, we're accountable for figuring out what that means for our life. There's no need for this to be stressful or fear based — as in, thinking we have to go through a certain set of motions to be "liked" by Spirit or to fulfill some sort of time requirement. To a degree, the more time we devote, the better we will get — but, on the flip side, if we devote so much time to Spirit, dedicating ourselves so completely that we become attached to it, it's usually a sign that ego and fear have taken hold.

If it's possible for you to meditate every day, that's awesome! I absolutely think that such a practice is good for most people. That said, *I don't even meditate every day*. It's true! I confess. If the same is true for you, don't worry; this section has you covered. Whether it's five days a week or once a week, I'll teach you how to leverage consistency as part of psychic development.

Spiritual connection can help regardless of our situation. During the years I spent at home when my kids were little, I wasn't really engaging in this work. I remember those years well, and I don't even know if it would have been possible to find time to meditate! I remember having to take time-outs to just breathe.

But taking a time-out to breathe, as it turns out, is a powerful way to start bringing a regular spiritual practice into your life. Looking back, I see that this *was* my spiritual connection at the time. We have to breathe all the time anyway, so we may as well show up for what's happening, right? Taking three deep breaths is a great start. To slow it down even more than that, we can add in a mantra: *I am breathing in. I am breathing out.* We can extend it to thirty seconds or a minute. Making a simple technique like this into habit can go a long way toward welcoming the shift to a more spiritual way of life.

Once we're in the habit of stopping to notice the breath several times a day, we can add in taking a pause to talk to Spirit. I like to start with a thank-you. I connect with the breath and then gratitude; it feels like a natural order. If I can connect to specific things that inspire gratitude, that helps, too. This is also a good moment to say, "I need help. Can you show me guidance?" — if we need it, that is.

This multistep process happens in a split second. It's the

same one — believing, asking, and acting — that I promoted in my first book. I think of this process as a little check-in with Spirit. Making it habitual shifts our life completely, or perhaps it marks a shift that is already taking place. Without adjusting our schedule at all, we've managed to program connecting with Spirit into our daily activities. Even the busiest person can do this.

It's important to understand this because modern culture suggests that a spiritual life is something flashy and outward. To be spiritual, at least according to Instagram, we need a pillow to meditate on, and preferably an ocean view, ideally from a bamboo platform at a jungle resort in Bali. It makes for a beautiful image, and potentially a profound meditation, but it's not very realistic for most people. When we build up this idealized image in our heads, we forget one of the most important truths about meditation, which is that the moment we feel that deep, unmistakable connection, it doesn't matter where we are or how long we'll stay. Spirit doesn't care where we are. No beach, no jungle platform, no problem.

Once we start checking in with Spirit, feeding our connection daily, we start to tap into what we really need in the moment. Our self-care game improves drastically, because Spirit was always trying to tell us when things were off, but now we're listening. One day, Spirit might tell us to go take a little walk. Or we might just intuit that today, we need to take our lunch break alone, even if that means we have to sit in our car in the parking lot to do it. When we remember to let Spirit in regularly, our guides have a chance to weigh in on what's happening more often. From that point on we can trust that they'll take it from there. After all, they are always ready to guide us — they're just waiting for the opportunity.

Many people start to find patterns around the way they connect with Spirit. For instance, in many traditions there is a gratitude practice tied to meals or some sort of prayer just before bed. I think both of these are good models. Personally, I've gravitated toward a fairly consistent morning practice. Shortly after waking up, I think, *Dear guides, with gratitude I ask that you fill my body and soul with your protection. I am ready to receive your messages and guidance. Please give me the clarity and compassion to serve with love and positivity.* I also smudge frequently, and at least once a day I ground myself and bring in the light, whether I make it more formal or just do it quickly, between activities. I let my intuition signal me when the time is right.

When I'm using my gifts a lot, I increase my prayers and check-ins, along with the amount of rest and downtime that allow me to avoid what I call a spiritual hangover — the fatigue, headaches, brain fog, and irritability that often accompany over-channeling. I also increase my meditation — this is usually natural, as Spirit often calls me to meditate more when things are intense — and exercise, as I find exercise really clears my head and puts me in my body. When I devote just a little effort to my spiritual well-being and connection, I find that Spirit amplifies the effects tenfold.

Spirit always shows up to support us when we dedicate ourselves to regular spiritual practice. As long as *we* consistently reach out, our Team can consistently get in to help. We're accountable for finding our own way, making our connection with Spirit feel authentic to us. Even if we're bringing in the light while we're in the shower, or we've got a kid on each hip so we're just listening to some mantra music and connecting with the breath, we find a way to fit Spirit into our routine, and over time, it just becomes instinctual. The more we check in with Spirit, the more opportunities we have to recognize what might help in the moment.

This also gives us the opportunity to allow our connection

with Spirit to morph and redirect itself over time, as needed. This is one of the main reasons I promote such a DIY relationship to spirituality: I trust your guides. I want you to trust them right now, today. And five years from now, if they need to tell you it's time to pick up a Tarot deck, or it's time to start communicating with animals, or it's time to channel ancestors in Spirit, I want you to be able to listen to that, too. If they indicate that one hour a day of meditation is going to help you — or if they recognize that's simply unattainable at this stage, so a five-minute meditation in the grocery-store parking lot is going to have to do — the goal is for you to receive that message and honor it. It's not worth it to me to teach anyone a certain formula for connecting with Spirit. That's not how it works. Each of us *makes* the formula on our own in each moment, with our own guides leading the way.

I've had students who sat down with oracle cards once a week because that's when their spouse could care for the kids. I've known people who meditate on the subway or on their lunch break. Many people add a spiritual component to their other habitual practices, like exercise, energy work, or studying spiritual books. It's very individual. It has to work *for you* in order for it to work.

Once we find the formula that works for us, the benefits of our spiritual practice begin to ripple out into our lives.

Shifting to a Spiritual Life

Committing to Spirit is the most empowering thing we can do for ourselves and our psychic development. It's life changing.

This was certainly true for me. Life turned into Technicolor when I began honoring Spirit daily. My confidence rose. Suddenly, I knew my place in the world. My relationships started to change — some shifted in form, and certain relationships began to fade away as new ones took their place. Things were dissolving, but I was calm. I realized that the aspects of my life and personality undergoing renovation were simply clearing space for what would serve me better.

At the heart of it, we all want to be the truest and most authentic version of ourselves. We know what it feels like to be in alignment with who we really are; we feel it in magical moments of connection, when we're in our element displaying our best talent or when we're relaxing with the people who love us the most. There's a confidence, a sense we're held, a feeling like we can do no wrong as long as we do our best. We feel a support beyond anything we could have ever imagined. Once we establish an ongoing relationship with Spirit and start feeding it in the little moments throughout our day, we can feel like that whenever we want. A relationship with Spirit is like a relationship with our deepest self. It's right there, accessible, waiting for us whenever we need it.

That doesn't mean we won't have problems. Stuff will come up; things will go wrong. We'll screw up some days and not know what the hell to do. I still don't turn to Spirit every time things don't go my way. Sometimes I just sit around and lament, like anyone else, complaining about how difficult my circumstances are to myself, my husband, and my friends. But as soon as I remember, I come back. I pause to take a breath or step outside, or I stop, go grab some sage, smudge myself, and search the recesses of my mind for some teeny tiny thing that inspires gratitude.

In the same way, there will still be moments when everything goes right and we forget to be grateful. We don't make the occasion spiritual in the least; instead, we drink a glass of wine, kick back, and celebrate. This, too, is part of life. It's OK! When we can, as soon as it occurs to us, we can acknowledge our guides and thank them for all they did to lead us to our good fortune.

Most of the time, however, we feel Spirit with us. This shift is so clear and undeniable that it makes it difficult to imagine we ever *didn't* operate with Spirit at our side. We trust so much more. It becomes easier to accept what comes our way because we know our Team is with us, guiding us. We can work and navigate through our personal problems in different, more constructive ways, solving them with much more ease. Our decision-making begins to connect more deeply to the greatest good of everyone involved, including ourselves.

This increases our self-esteem, which increases our self-care. It helps us honor our own boundaries and helps others — those in our lives and those in Spirit — honor our boundaries, too.

Ariela, whom I first wrote about in chapter 2, went through a massive transformation when she committed to her spiritual life. At first, she was worried about being judged. I watched her shed her fear like a snake's skin, and soon thereafter she started channeling messages live, connecting with her guides every day so she could be of service to the world. This changed her life drastically. Interpersonal relationships that she had struggled with for years immediately made sense; self-destructive behaviors became easier to recognize; for the first time in her young life, she began to gain agency over her circumstances. This is precisely the strength and fortitude that a spiritual life can give us, if we're only brave enough to commit to it.

PRACTICE

·· ·)◦(· ··

One-Week Spiritual Schedule

Creating a strong spiritual schedule is an important way we can support our psychic development. It's an outer framework that represents the process happening inside of us, the turning inward toward Spirit that is naturally taking place. Throughout this chapter, we've discussed the value of an informal, personalized habit of turning to Spirit. Here, we're backing that up with an experiment in commitment. We're playing with the idea of formalizing our spiritual practice.

Some students end up doing this exercise once and never again. They do not feel a pull to practice in this way. Others feel really drawn to it; it helps them lend order to their days and maintain a connection. They might set a long-term schedule and stick to it or do this exercise every single week if their schedule is more adaptable. Still others let this practice go for months or even years, coming back to it when life throws them a curveball and connecting with their Team feels difficult. Whether it calls you or not, this is a good practice to have in your toolbox.

Start by creating your schedule for just a week. Go slow and be easy on yourself, putting simple goals on the calendar each day. You want some slam dunks in there — things you know you can achieve. As you'll see in the examples below, there are achievable goals to match every schedule; none of this needs to take much time, if time doesn't feel available. To do this exercise, you may want a journal and a pen. You may also want to program your schedule into your smartphone calendar or raid the craft closet to make a glittery, sparkly version to put up on the wall. Do it your way, but the most important thing is that you write down achievable goals and follow through on them. Let these examples serve as a guide.

Example 1: Lori

Lori is super dedicated to her spiritual practice! She and her husband have meditated together every morning for over a decade. They sometimes allow themselves to skip meditation on Sundays or if they are sick, but that's it. Lori has been working to develop her gifts as a medium for many years. She is self-employed as a healer, her kids are out of the home, and she is grateful to finally have abundant time for her spiritual practice. In addition to what's listed below, Lori practices cleansing and grounding daily. She also picks an oracle card every morning, leaving it on her altar until she replaces it the following day. Lori takes in-person mediumship classes every week, and at least once a month she signs up for an online workshop. She has an active social life, and since many of her friends are also on the path to psychic development, she makes a point of trading a practice session twice a week, too.

Lori's Schedule

	MON	TUES	WED	THURS	FRI	SAT	SUN
Morning	5:30–6:30 Meditation 6:30–6:45 Journaling 6:45–7:10 Yoga	5:30–6:30 Meditation 6:30–6:45 Journaling 6:45–7:10 Yoga	5:30–6:30 Meditation 6:30–6:45 Journaling 6:45–7:10 Yoga	5:30–6:30 Meditation 6:30–6:45 Journaling 6:45–7:10 Yoga	5:30–6:30 Meditation 6:30–6:45 Journaling 6:45–7:10 Yoga	One-hour guided meditation Extended grounding practice Automatic writing	One-hour meditation
Afternoon			Practicing trade with Suzanne			3:00–6:00 Online crystals workshop	Practicing trade with Li
Evening	Automatic writing Reading and prayers	7:00–8:30 Mediumship class Reading and prayers	Reading and prayers	7:00–8:30 Mediumship class Reading and prayers	Reading and prayers	Reading and prayers	5:30–7:00 Restorative yoga class Reading and prayers

Example 2: Tom

Tom works full-time running a company from his home office, and his workweeks are very busy. He lives alone, and his school-age son Jonah joins him most weekends. Tom is new to psychic development, but he is progressing quickly. I suspect that this is in part because as a runner, he is very adept at clearing his mind. Athletics, and running in particular, is such an important part of Tom's practice of connection that he includes it on his spiritual schedule. For Tom, exercise is a crucial form of self-care that allows him to focus and connect with Spirit. He also practices a mantra meditation with a group once a week and repeats it on his own at least twice more, smudging himself with incense as part of the ritual. Some members of the same group meet for a book club on Sundays, which he joins whenever he can. Tom describes himself as "not a morning person," but he has trained himself to recite a small prayer calling in his guides to support him before getting out of bed.

Tom's Schedule

	MON	TUES	WED	THURS	FRI	SAT	SUN
Morning	Prayer	Prayer	Prayer	Prayer	Prayer	Prayer	Prayer Reading hour with Jonah
Afternoon	Walk during lunch hour	Reading during lunch hour	Walk during lunch hour	Reading during lunch hour	Walk during lunch hour		
Evening	5:30–6:15 Run 8:00–8:45 Meditation	5:30–6:15 Run Spiritual podcast with dinner	5:30–6:15 Run 8:00–8:45 Meditation	5:30–6:15 Run Spiritual podcast with dinner	5:30–6:15 Run 8:00–8:45 Meditation	4:30–5:30 Weight room 5:30–6:15 Run	5:30–6:15 Run 7:30–9:00 Spiritual book group

Example 3: Anita

A decade ago, Anita was super engaged in her spiritual practice. She read, went to workshops, and meditated. Today, she is a wife and mother. She works Monday, Wednesday, and Friday in retail, and ever since her twins were born, her forty-five-minute commute is some of the only time she gets to herself. On Tuesday and Thursday she is at home alone with her infant daughters, and she and her husband like to take them hiking with the dog on the weekends. On Sunday, she and her mother go to church. The vast majority of Anita's spiritual practice involves checking in with her breath as often as she can. *She uses her breaks at work to listen to an uplifting song or sit in silence for a few minutes, and she communicates with her guides throughout her day as she navigates parenting. When she struggles with a difficult decision, Anita reaches for her pendulum or her oracle cards, and one Saturday a month she springs for childcare and attends an intuitive workshop online where she can practice reading for others.*

Anita's Schedule

	MON	TUES	WED	THURS	FRI	SAT	SUN
Morning	Grounding practice (shower) Spiritual podcast (commute)	Grounding practice (shower)	Grounding practice (shower) Spiritual podcast (commute)	Grounding practice (shower)	Grounding practice (shower) Spiritual podcast (commute)	Prayer Grounding practice (shower)	Grounding practice (shower) Church
Afternoon	Music (commute)	Reading during lunch hour	Music (commute)	Five-minute breath check-in after lunch	Music (commute)	Silence (if no one cries!), hike, or intuitive workshop	
Evening	15-minute meditation before bed	Spiritual music, podcast, or silence during dog walk	15-minute meditation before bed	Spiritual music, podcast, or silence during dog walk	15-minute meditation before bed		Spiritual music, podcast, or silence during dog walk
Notes	*Remember to check in with Spirit during breaks	*Don't forget to put on spiritual music in emergencies!	*Remember to check in with Spirit during breaks	*Don't forget to put on spiritual music in emergencies!	*Remember to check in with Spirit during breaks		

As you can see in the examples above, a spiritual schedule can take many forms. Some people live very scheduled lives, while others do not; some people thrive with structure, while others do much better living spontaneously in the moment. In the first example above, Lori has a good deal of control over her schedule and is often in a position to choose how she spends her time. Tom has less control because he's so busy, though he still has a good deal of time to himself. Anita has very little time to herself, but she makes the most of what she can get. By reminding herself to check in with Spirit frequently, she's managing to keep in regular contact with her guides during these busy years.

Notice that none of these schedules is better than the others. They are all "right." The regular, consistent connection with Spirit is what makes this technique effective.

Once you've finished your schedule, try it out! Just do one week at first. If you can't meet your commitments, journal about why not, or ask your guides as part of an automatic-writing practice. If you need to adjust your spiritual schedule and try again, do it. This is an experiment. You're welcome to use this exercise every week for the rest of your life or never again — it's your process, so you are in charge!

Living a Spiritual Life

Through exploring a spiritual schedule, we start to give structure to this natural shift toward a spiritual life that is already taking place. This is a necessary and important step in the journey of any developing psychic. However we choose to approach it, at some point each one of us moves away from playing with spirituality and toward a real, working relationship. It's a bit of a transition, but after mentoring many students through the process, I'm confident that you'll find your way. And I'm certain that doing so will be a game changer for the rest of your spiritual life.

When we stop dabbling and really commit to living a life with Spirit, we give ourselves the foundation we need to stay balanced. We'll have a stronger baseline, making it easier to identify when we're feeling out of sorts or just "off." And when we make that identification, our next move will be automatic: more often than not, we'll turn to Spirit without stopping to think about it. Consistent, regular spiritual practice — whatever that looks like for us — is what allows us to respond appropriately. It's our barometer. It's what signals to us that it's time to get back into balance.

Chapter Eight

GET BALANCED

*Integrating Divine Guidance
into Everyday Life*

O nce connecting with our guides and asking for spiritual
support becomes a reflex, it's time to start devoting conscious attention to finding balance in our lives.

The previous seven techniques have all been dedicated to
helping you find a structure for your relationship with Spirit.
Each of us can work with these ideas to find our own way to an
ongoing supportive relationship with creative Source, or God,
or whatever name we give to the concept of the divine mystery
that unites life. Once we've done this, our next step is to find
our own way to sustain it. Ideally, our intuitive life fits within
the framework of the rest of our life quite comfortably. From
there, it informs us as professionals, partners, family members,

and friends. It affects the way we treat finances, our career, household affairs, and our own bodies. If we can make it sustainable, spiritual connection with our own higher guidance can bring a joyful dimension to everything we do.

This chapter is all about that long-term sustainability, which is only possible when we consciously focus on balancing the many aspects of our world, including guidance from our Team. We'll start by looking at what balance means in this context (as well as what it doesn't). Then we'll consider how we can know when we're out of balance and how we can find it again. At the end of the chapter, I'll offer you a practice to help you assess and correct your balance whenever you feel even the slightest bit "off."

When we are able to sustain a connection with Spirit and keep our lives in balance, our intuitive abilities gain the fertile ground they need to truly flourish. Getting balanced includes setting boundaries and reassessing priorities. It is intuitive and dynamic. And it's absolutely key to our ability to move through the physical world while honoring the psychic world, too.

Balancing Our World

Spiritual teachers and traditions frequently use the concept of balance to refer to a variety of things. When I write about balance, I'm referring to balancing our physical body, our spiritual body, our mental body, and our emotional body. Together, these form our total being. The goal is to assess the various aspects of our lives and find balance between them, thereby aligning our soul with its greatest potential.

This assessing-and-balancing technique is helpful because it's the factor that allows us to remain completely connected to Spirit, accessing guidance when we need it throughout our day, while still living in the world. Sure, there are people who feel called to go spend the rest of their lives meditating in a cave, and if you are one of them, I encourage you to follow that guidance. But for the rest of us — the ones whose lives include taking kids to soccer practice every Tuesday, going to the office on weekdays from 9 to 5, gathering for family reunions, and volunteering at an animal shelter or doing whatever it is that brings us joy that isn't specifically "psychic activity" — balance is essential. This is even (and perhaps especially) true for those who integrate their intuitive practice into their social and/or professional lives. As I deepened my intuitive work, launching myself as a working psychic medium, balance became even more important to me. The same is true for many of my students, regardless of whether they go pro: to reach their full intuitive potential, they have to find and maintain balance.

I like to think of getting balanced as tending to a large set of spinning plates on the ends of poles, like in a circus act. When someone is out of balance — or, more often than not, when that someone is me — I see one of the plates begin to wobble. Spinning a bunch of plates at once is an active, dynamic process. Balance isn't something we achieve one time; we don't just tick the "get balanced" box off our spiritual to-do list and call it good. Getting balanced means assessing and adjusting on an ongoing basis. It's a constant motion, a regular negotiation between ourselves and the various aspects of our lives. It's a learning process.

While we're learning to spin numerous plates at once, it's a given that some plates are going to drop. That's part of learning. A dropped plate isn't a failure but an inevitability. Our work, then, is to develop the resources to allow us to pick up the plate quickly and get it spinning again. We aren't responsible for being flawless; instead, it's up to us to do our best, to try to keep pace with our plates and respond effectively when they fall. Knowing this takes the pressure off. It allows us to focus on the endeavor of *trying* to keep the plates going without getting attached to perfection.

So what are the plates? In this analogy, the plates represent the different aspects of our lives. This includes the roles we play in relation to other people as well as the way we spend our days — the ideas and activities that engage us as we go through our lives. Work and career usually comprises one plate, parenthood another, romance and partnership another, and so forth. Our homelife is its own plate, as is our actual home — the environment we have created to spend so much time in. Our relationship to the earth is as well. Our physical body includes its own set of small plates, like exercise, sleep, and nutrition. Friendship and recreation are plates. Quietude and creativity are, too.

Our balance can therefore be measured by the health of *our relationship to* each of these areas. Note here that I'm not referring to everything going right in each of these areas. I'm not referring to everything being easy or devoid of problems. This is a common misconception about balance: the idea that being in balance means everything goes our way. Instead, as I understand balance, it refers to our ability to attune to and address what we need in any given moment. When we're in balance, we feel that we're right with Spirit. We're in alignment. We're tending to what is important to us; we're creating and maintaining a joyful existence. Our lives may not be perfect — in fact, it's pretty likely they aren't! — but our souls are fed. This is how it feels when our beautiful plates are spinning nice and flat, like we have healthy, meaningful relationships with the world around us.

Once we get all our plates spinning, our focus can shift to keeping them that way. It's important to notice that this is, in essence, an impossible task — that like so many of the other techniques in this book, such as working with ego, fear, and boundaries, balance is an ongoing pursuit. We're here, we're learning lessons, and sometimes we're learning them the hard way. If we can stabilize ourselves enough to find balance, however, we can start to progress more steadily. We may be able to use our intuition to recognize a little bit sooner that one of our plates is beginning to wobble than we would have in the past — this is a huge victory! We can tap into our intuition, which tells us there is something important in our lives that needs tending and attention. We may even begin to rescue our plates, catching and righting them the second before they fall.

To do this, it helps to understand how and when plates fall. Often the thing that allows one plate to fall is focusing too much on another. We lean in, trying to get one plate spinning just right, not noticing that the plate behind us is terribly out of whack. It's also common for us to intentionally look away from a wobbling plate; perhaps realizing that an area of our lives isn't really working brings us too much anxiety, or maybe we just feel too exhausted to deal with it. We let the plate wobble and wobble, ignoring what's happened, and we're not really surprised to see it come crashing down — we just didn't know what to do about it.

Sometimes, a plate falling can block our spiritual connection — not in a scary, long-term way but in a temporary, hey-wake-up sort of way. This is often actually our own guides trying to get our attention to tell us where and how we need to put in work.

Accepting Guidance

By now, you know that your guides are always with you. You've explored many of the ways they're trying to communicate with you; your connection is deepening. Hopefully, you feel confident that your guides have your back and are always doing what's in your highest interest, even when you don't understand all the details.

If so, you're prepared to hear something a little more advanced about guidance: sometimes, it comes in through challenge. This is tricky, because by no means do I want to imply that our guides are punitive. They aren't here to punish us or tell us we're wrong. But every once in a while they will let us become uncomfortable in a certain area of our lives, or around a certain issue, in order to get us to pay attention to it.

Remember, we're worldly beings. Yes, we are infinite souls, but those souls are housed right here in these very human bodies. We exist in the world, and because of this, we have to pay attention to the world. Discomfort is a tool Spirit uses to communicate with us. When blocks, setbacks, disappointments, or conflict show up in our world, it's up to us to ask, *What are my guides trying to show me? What needs more attention here? Am I moving on without addressing something? Am I not giving enough energy to this area of my life?*

Our guides want us in balance for very practical reasons. When I don't pay enough attention to my body — which usually means not getting enough exercise, something instrumental to my spiritual well-being — I start to feel mentally fatigued. When I feel fatigued mentally, how can I channel spiritually? It's not possible.

This is true when we aren't paying enough attention to areas of our lives and also when we're paying *too much* attention. Many students start to overdo things spiritually at first. I get it — developing psychic gifts is exciting! But when we leave everything else just sitting there neglected, when we try to read every single day or pull a card for every single question that arises in our lives, when we think every answer has to come in through a certain avenue or in a certain way, it's just not right. Spiritually overdoing it — just like being a workaholic or a helicopter parent or obsessing over your relationship — isn't balanced behavior. It's exhausting. Over time, it's as draining of spiritual energy as any other imbalance. Our guides want to spare us this, so sometimes, when we overdo things spiritually, they just cut us off.

This can show up as radio silence in meditation. It can also show up as canceled appointments. I had a strong experience with this one time when I scheduled far too many readings in a month. As the end of the month approached, my clairs exhausted, I kept hearing that I should cancel a specific appointment. I blew these urgings off as laziness; I knew I was tired, but I thought I could just push through. "No," my guides pleaded with me. "That one, on Thursday, the one with the woman in Staten Island. Cancel it!" I didn't. Sure enough, Thursday rolled around, and the woman from Staten Island and I hopped on the phone in our scheduled time slot. She was very nice, nothing wrong with her, no problems at all. She asked her question sincerely and ... *nothing*. Crickets. I couldn't hear a word. I checked my other senses, grasping for anything, but my guides were mum. I apologized and got off the phone, refunding what she'd paid.

Nowadays, I don't let things get to that point. If my Team tells me to cancel, I cancel; it's awkward, but I push past the awkwardness to honor my own balance. For instance, I've been working a lot lately. I'm running various programs, offering several private readings a week, mentoring students, and writing a book — *help!* I've spoken with my guides, and they're supporting it to a point, but they've given me a cutoff date. "You can do this, but you're going to need a break," they've told me. "We'll support you doing this up until this point, and no more." I've marked the date on my calendar and cleared the entire week following it. I *will* be taking a break. It's their job to tell me — and it's my job to honor what they say.

Sometimes, Spirit even lines things up to help us get back into balance. For instance, they'll prompt a deep conversation in a relationship where communication is not going well, or they'll cause a momentary financial freak-out to help us realize our money-management strategy needs an update. I've even seen them mess with the workplace, orchestrating a dreaded layoff when we need to quit our job, or a really nasty project to get us in our superior's office asking for the raise we've deserved all along. They'll bring up a problem in the family just to get us in the house more.

Once you understand this, the question becomes: Are you listening? When issues or drama come up in your life, can you widen your focus for a moment and understand what, if anything, your guides are trying to say? They aren't always trying to say something — sometimes, stuff just happens. (Remember, overdoing spirituality by reading meaning into absolutely everything in life isn't balanced!) But are you willing to entertain the question? Getting balanced requires us to pay close attention to our lives, being open to the possibility that the challenges we face are forms of communication from our Team — without clinging to that as absolute truth.

Rachel is one of my more advanced students. She quickly progressed from casually developing her intuition to full-on psychic mediumship. While she maintains a full-time job in the medical profession, she books readings in the evenings after work. I act as a sort of supervisor for this work, mentoring her through the process of offering her gifts professionally. Rachel is also a new mom. On a phone call during her third trimester of pregnancy, my guides showed me an image of her absolutely exhausted, drained of all energy.

"Are you tired?" I asked.

"Am I ever!" she answered.

I asked how many readings she was doing a week and was shocked by the number. "Are your guides leading you to do that much?" I asked.

"Actually, no," she responded, "I received a download that I should cut a few appointments this week, but I love reading so much! I think it will be OK."

I encouraged her to reschedule some of her appointments to keep herself balanced, spreading them out over more time so she had space to rest and recover between readings. If her guides had suggested it, I knew it was important.

A few weeks later, Rachel sent an emergency text. We hopped on the phone right away. She was devastated; her last few readings had been fuzzy, not sharp, and it had been hard to connect with her sitters. Her confidence was shaken. She wondered why she was even reading at all. The more emotionally worked up she became, the murkier the guidance she received. "It's like I have no idea what they want from me!" she said, frustrated. I listened compassionately for a few minutes before breaking in.

"What about that thing about spreading out your appointments?" I asked gently. Rachel mumbled something in response. It turned out she hadn't rescheduled a single one. I explained that she was overdoing it. She was over-reading and ignoring her guides. Her body was busy making a human being (no small task, as I remember it), her mind was busy with her day job, and the quantity of time she was devoting to intuitive work was actually diminishing its quality. I explained that this wasn't just my opinion but the message I believed her guides were trying to convey all along, and I shared my own experience with the client from Staten Island.

By the end of the call, Rachel was out of her emotional tailspin and we were laughing at the silly, bullheaded way we all resist guidance sometimes. Sure enough, when Rachel cut back on reading for others, her connection to Spirit returned. She found a healthy new balance for the rest of her pregnancy. Now that her child is growing older, her guides are leading her to shift her practice and find balance again — and this time, Rachel is listening.

Over time, I learned to marry my free will to my guidance. That means that when I receive a message from my Team, I use my free will to follow it. I don't fight it anymore. I just say "Thank you!" and follow the instructions I'm given. I love my guides and appreciate their input; I try to respond when it's just a whisper, but when they have to speak a little louder for me to hear, I'm OK with that, too.

Falling Plates

Let's return to the idea of spinning plates. When a plate comes crashing down, it can make a big mess. That means that when our guides suggest we pay attention to an area of our lives and we miss the message, freeze up, or otherwise fail to respond, they can send us bigger issues — ones that are *sure* to get our attention. While we don't need to motivate ourselves out of fear of this, the awareness helps. It reminds us that balance is an integral part of self-care.

Imbalance often manifests physically. In my case, I dealt with chronic bronchitis for several years. The doctors couldn't figure out exactly what was causing it, and it got to the point where they wanted me to take a preventive medication. I inherently felt that the cause was spiritual; it was early in my work as a psychic medium, and I could feel that I was putting too much energy into my spiritual life and not enough into the rest of my life. I started reducing the number of appointments I made and turning my energy back toward my important relationships. At one point, between bouts of bronchitis, I broke a vocal cord. This helped me see that I had room to grow in terms of my communication. I learned to deal with my emotions more directly, communicate what I needed to share right away, and have the difficult conversations I had spent years avoiding.

It's worth noting that I also had other injuries and illnesses during these years. I had colds that just felt like colds; I pulled a muscle at the gym, which I'm pretty sure was just a pulled muscle at the gym. Not everything that happens to us physically is a sign from our guides, although some things can be. (In either case, if you have a medical concern, please consult a physician.) It's important to understand this, because absolutist thinking can lead us to hold ourselves accountable for things that have nothing to do with us, and perhaps even dip into accountability's unhealthy, shadowy manifestation: self-blame. The difference between a health issue that is physical in nature and one that is spiritual in nature is hard to assess from the outside. It's a felt difference, one that comes in mostly through intuition.

Often, the plate that falls can show us exactly where we need to pay more attention. Our homelife explodes in argument, or our career takes a sudden bad turn, demonstrating our lack of balance in that area. A literal interpretation is all we need to make sense of the message we're given. The plate falls precisely because we weren't tending to that area, and this jolts us awake.

Other times, the falling plate is a more obscure reference to what's wrong. Sometimes it's metaphoric — a scare with the heart pointing toward keeping the heart open, *not* a lack of attention to cardiac health, or a financial issue cropping up to show us wounds in our relationship with safety and security, *not* to indicate that we need to put more into savings. And like the colds and pulled muscles I noted above, it sometimes doesn't "mean" anything at all. One of my dear friends, whom we all call Captain Sunshine, is going through cancer treatments. An easy interpretation would be that she "attracted" her cancer, but I simply do not believe this is the case — she's one of the most positive people I know! Through our conversations, Captain Sunshine has seen that her work is to take this blamey, negative version of accountability out of the picture and instead look at why her body went out of balance and what she can do to correct the balance today. This is a tricky distinction, and in the end, it's not for anyone else to decide. Each one of us gets to choose what meaning we make or don't make of challenges like these.

In almost all cases, we actually know exactly where and how we're out of balance. It may be buried down pretty deep in there, but we know. Maybe there's a particular health issue we're avoiding, or our bank account is nearing empty, or our marriage has taken a serious downturn, and we're just ignoring it. We're looking away, unable to face what's happening, or we're only vaguely aware that we're seeing things from a too-narrow viewpoint. When something goes wrong, when a plate comes crashing down, whether it's related to the thing we're ignoring or not, we know what we need to do. At that point, we're accountable for just being humble about it, understanding that everybody's learning something.

That means that even when we commit ourselves to finding balance and allowing the experience to largely be informed by our Team, the interpretation piece is still up to us. We're still accountable for making sense of what our guides are trying to tell us about balance. They may point us to all sorts of activities: maybe it's starting a difficult conversation, or writing a letter, or doing a forgiveness meditation five mornings in a row, or getting to the gym, or starting on a new supplement, or trying a new medication, or making a doctor's appointment. When we direct our free will to follow the guidance we receive *reflexively* — when we make our response automatic — we don't even have to interpret what it means. Did going for a run yesterday prevent a plate from falling? Maybe. Did *not* signing up for that spiritual workshop, opting to spend a Saturday morning with the kids instead, keep another plate in the air? It could be, but that isn't our business. To make our relationship with Spirit sustainable, we just keep listening and responding the best we can — even when we don't know why. We just try to keep those plates spinning.

This is an ongoing, lifelong pursuit, as I've said. The following practice can help you get started.

PRACTICE

Finding Your Balance

This practice involves connecting with your guides to see where you're out of balance.

You'll do so through automatic writing. As always, I encourage you to make this process your own. I've provided suggestions, but if other questions or ideas come to you, the sky is the limit! Many intuitives use automatic writing frequently in their practice, and I urge you to explore *your* technique, finding the way that works best for you.

There are two things I suggest to everyone: First, take enough time to do this. We often get the impulse to automatic-write but then start questioning ourselves, which leads us to get only the beginning of the transmission. Second, to prevent this, keep your pen moving the entire time. Just keep going, even if you think it's nonsense. Making this a habit will train your brain to not question what you receive. You may shift handwriting, energy, use of language as you go — roll with it. You may even change guides within the same writing. You may know exactly who you are channeling, or you may not (though if you want to channel someone specific, writing the name of a loved one — or of a guide if you know it — at the top of the page can help).

This particular automatic-writing exercise has several steps, and I encourage you to go through them back-to-back, in a single sitting. You'll need at least twenty minutes to do so. You'll also want a journal, a pen, and a timer.

Start by writing a specific guide's name at the top, if appropriate, or you can just generally direct it to all your guides with your intention.

Question 1

First, you'll identify the areas of your life that are out of balance. Write one of the following questions:

- *Where am I out of balance?*
- *What am I missing?*
- *How am I out of alignment?*

Set a timer for five minutes and freewrite. Keep your pen moving the whole time.

When you finish, read what you wrote aloud. It's important to hear the words spoken, so please don't skip this step, even if it feels silly! Reading aloud is a fantastic way to receive guidance on a deeper level.

Look back at what you wrote — which may be anything from a

list to beautiful poetry to a scrawling, scribbly mess — and study it for themes, such as family, work, or health. Then, below your automatic writing, clearly list the themes you find.

Question 2

Next, you'll look at what you're doing to contribute to the issue. Here, you'll discover the actions your guides want you to stop doing in order to find balance. Write one of the following questions:

- *What am I doing to contribute to this imbalance?*
- *What actions could I avoid in order to address the imbalance in ____ [theme]?*
- *What pattern do I need to stop falling into?*

Again, set your timer and write for five more minutes. When you finish, look at both your lists. You may notice a negative slant to your answers, such as "Eating processed sugar," "Staying in my comfort zone," or "Judging my friends." It's often easier for us to think in the negative. There's nothing inherently wrong with that, but Spirit works in the positive, so we're best served if we flip these ideas around. Next to any negative answer, write down its positive, solution-oriented equivalent, such as "Eat more fruit," "Try new things," or "Appreciate my friends more."

Question 3

Now you'll further consider where you need to start taking action. Write one of the following questions:

- *What do I need to do?*
- *What actions could I take to address the imbalance in ____ [theme]?*
- *How can I move myself back toward balance?*

Set your timer for five minutes and freewrite again. This time, as you download, push for specific details — the more specific, the better. Set the clear intention that you want guidance that involves action.

When you're finished, read your answers to questions 2 and 3 aloud. Again, please don't skip this! Then, if your next steps aren't already quite obvious, distill your download into a set of practical actions you can take or behaviors you could change. Examples include: "Set up a doctor's appointment," "Start meditating for ten minutes in the mornings," "Replace my repetitive thoughts with a mantra," and "Sign up for a dance class."

Then, to the degree that it's possible, commit to each action here and now. For example, get out your phone and schedule the doctor's appointment, or set an alarm to remind you to meditate. If you need to automatic-write in the mornings, put your journal and a pen next to your bed, or if you need to join a certain class, start looking for one that might suit you. Be sure to get any important dates and times onto your schedule and to find the funds you might need, reallocating, saving, or fundraising as necessary. I encourage you to not shy away from these logistical details; they're an essential part of living a balanced life on Earth.

Sustaining a Balanced Life

Finding and maintaining balance between the spiritual, emotional, physical, and mental bodies is crucial if we want our spiritual life to be sustainable long-term. This commitment to balance allows us to remain deeply connected to the realm of Spirit while keeping our feet firmly planted on the physical plane. It helps us become portals of the light, bringing Source energy right here and spreading it around the world. This is our most sacred mission as intuitives.

Beyond that, the details of the mission vary from person

to person. Each of us is accountable for finding our own way to share the light we receive. Whether it's as a psychic medium, a healer, a teacher, a parent, an animal communicator, or anything else, the role of bringing the divine light to Earth is a sacred business. It's up to us to find our own unique service.

Chapter Nine

GO FORTH AND SERVE

Putting the Lessons into Action

O nce you've stopped dabbling in spirituality and have found a way to balance it with the rest of your life, the call to service becomes clearer. It may be that up to this point, you have primarily been interested in using your spirituality for your own purposes. Or you may have already started to hear the call to service at some point in the process. Or you may have even started this journey *because* of your call to service; perhaps the desire to help others has been flowing through you all along. Whatever your situation, once conversing with your Team becomes a regular part of your life, it's inevitable that you'll want to pay that forward somehow.

There are many ways to go about doing just that. Some

people will go on to be professional psychic mediums. Others will be healers, teachers, or artists. Still others will never monetize their spiritual gifts, preferring to infuse lightwork into other professional endeavors or simply into life itself. No matter how we go about it, we're accountable for exercising our free will to unlock what Spirit wants for us. Enacting our purpose involves connecting to our gifts and putting them in service of the greater good.

Service comes in so many forms. The easiest is to simply pay forward whatever we ourselves have received. We often miss that part — it's just easier to notice the types of service that are larger and more official, or that are put on a public platform. The most important form of service, however, is the one that's right for us.

This chapter will walk you through the process of seeking out how to best enact the divine will here on Earth. We'll look at different ways to go pro with your psychic gifts, as well as ways to integrate channeled wisdom into other forms of service. Then we'll consider how you can know you're serving in the best possible way. Understanding this is an essential piece of aligning yourself with your highest purpose.

Being of service is the best feeling in the world, one that has brought me more joy than I could ever describe. It's what Spirit wants for us; it's our birthright. Each one of us is blessed with the opportunity to serve, spreading our light far and wide. We are the ones accountable for what we choose to do with that opportunity.

Formal Psychic Service

I found myself serving almost by accident. For me, there wasn't a single event to mark my passage into formal psychic service; it was a steady flow from one life into another. Spirit took me gradually, really giving me a lot of time to think about it. People asked me for readings, and I just said yes.

It started in classes. I began to access my confidence, and my readings became exact. Other students started calling me and then referring me to their friends. I drove all over Long Island giving readings in people's homes. Over time, that turned into giving readings in restaurants and at psychic expos and eventually into giving group readings. It all went by word of mouth. I kept getting phone calls, I kept doing readings, and eventually, I was a full-blown professional psychic medium.

In that way, I have always been driven by service. I do this because I have been asked to do this. Of course, my free will is involved; I like things on a grand scale, and I never half-ass anything of importance. I admit that I half-ass plenty of things that I don't deem important, but when I set a goal, I don't mess around. When I played basketball, I was a starting center; when I was managing retail stores, I ran the flagship store; when my kids were young, I was a stay-at-home mom who chaperoned field trips and was on the school board. That's just my personality! I know how to focus and work hard, and I place a high value on achievement. Yet when it comes to mediumship, I was always motivated by service because I started with service. In other words, much of my skill set was developed because it was requested or required.

This is true for most of my students when they enter formal, and in many cases professional, psychic service. Keri, the medium and healer whom I mentioned in the introduction and chapter 4, started getting calls much like I did. We both responded to requests from people who came to us, asking to receive our gifts, and we slowly built a career out of that. Sometimes Spirit tells people to go into psychic service, too. A guide might suggest we serve in a specific way, which we pick up intuitively. This was the case for Ariela, who uploads messages to YouTube and livestreams channeling sessions, as I described in chapters 2 and 7. She quickly found resonance for her specific gift online.

In all cases, we enter into formal psychic service because, on some level, *this is what is asked of us*. I want to make that point clear because that's part of what makes it service!

There are many forms of formal service that involve psychic channeling. Some people are called to work with cards or mediumship, while others guide clients as coaches or counselors. Many visual artists are highly intuitive, and they channel the initial visions they draw, paint, sculpt, or design. Musicians often receive riffs, melodies, or entire songs through their psychic ear and then work to reproduce these so others can hear them, too. Writers, actors, and filmmakers channel to connect more deeply to their subjects. Storytellers download entire characters, scenes, and stories. Teachers and special-education workers can use their talents to intuit the unspoken needs of others, thus meeting these needs more fully. Nearly all healers, including bodyworkers, energy workers, alternative practitioners, doctors, and nurses, tap into their intuition to meet their patients' needs to some degree — even if it's not to diagnose or treat but just to figure out how they can communicate most effectively. In all these professional fields, intuitive information plays a major role.

It also plays a role for those who often find themselves offering personal advice in a professional capacity. One of my students, Julia, is a hairdresser. Like many hairdressers, she hears a lot of stories and is frequently in a position to give advice — on anything from relationships to career decisions to resolving disputes among friends. Her clients love her advice. They've come to trust her insight. It was only after consciously opening a conversation with Spirit that Julia realized much of what she offers is, in fact, channeled; part of the reason her clients keep asking her for advice is that it's so often spot-on!

We can choose to be transparent about the fact that we're integrating psychic information into our profession — or not. The degree to which we're up-front about our formal psychic service is often up to us. As we discussed in chapter 6, disclosing the origin of the information we share isn't always helpful and is sometimes entirely unnecessary. While this decision is up to each of us, it can help, once again, to frame it around *what's being asked*. Does this need to be said right now? Does the person hearing it want to hear it? Is this going to help the information land, or create resistance? It's not about being shady or secretive here. It's about recognizing that people download psychic input all the time, and while from one angle that is truly miraculous, from another it's not actually that big a deal. Serving means being egoless; it means delivering without fanfare. Sometimes that includes not mentioning the psychic origin of the information we share.

And sometimes we share that information in even less formal ways — ones that have nothing to do with our professional lives.

Serving Informally

Many forms of service are more informal. Here, I refer to channeling guidance through our relationships with others, with our own thoughts, and with life itself. We can bring channeled information, downloaded ideas, or psychic advice into all aspects of our lives. We can allow the guidance of Spirit to ripple out into all that we do.

Life is service. How we choose to classify and clarify it for ourselves reflects the dialogue we're having with Spirit. To truly serve, many of us have to dissolve our rigid ideas around what service is. When we realize just how often we are — or could be — serving, we gain a new respect for our role in things, for what we are really giving to the world.

Our Team always sends us messages of love. Even when they're asking us to do something difficult or challenging, they're doing it out of love. They're acting not only in our own best interest but in the best interest of everyone involved. That means when we truly align with them and start enacting their wishes here on Earth, we're automatically going to become kinder, more empathetic, more understanding, and more generous. Service is going to start popping up in the form of a kind phone call or text to someone at just the right moment. Our guides might push us to volunteer in an elderly care facility or to work with small children. We might feel called to give random gifts or donate philanthropically. All our psychic channeling may simply lead us to become a better friend, the one others come to for advice when they're most vulnerable. Like Julia the hairdresser, students frequently tell me that the people in their lives appreciate the channeled advice they receive and come back for more. It's valuable to them, even if they don't know it's channeled.

Often those who walk this path begin to serve through prayer. Similar to a grounding practice, praying becomes a quick, automatic response to everyday stressors. I have deep admiration for those who dedicate themselves to a consistent, regular practice of praying — those who don't just say, "I'll pray for you," but who actually do it, even if it's only for a moment. That's all it takes. Everyone who prays for the well-being of this world — regardless of where, how, for how long, or to whom they pray — is contributing to the positive energy on this planet. They are offering a beautiful act of service.

Others find their service beyond the human realm. Many gardeners will tell you they "talk" to their gardens, and we've all met someone with a green thumb — an uncanny knack for knowing what plants need. Communicating with animals is a common psychic gift. My student Sharon struggled when she first started taking classes because she knew she was psychic, but her readings weren't as accurate as she thought they would be. I began questioning her, trying to ascertain where she felt most open to receiving instruction from her Team. Sharon shared how she frequently worked with her pets, intuiting their energetic needs and healing them with her hands. I encouraged her to continue with this. Before long, Sharon started working with rescue dogs, reading them to determine everything from their dietary needs to the behavioral interventions that would be most effective. She signed up for a program wherein she was certified to train and rehabilitate rescue dogs. Today, Sharon has expanded her services to include matching families with the rescue dogs that will be best for them.

It took time for Sharon to figure out how to channel her service into the world. It required an ongoing process of self-inquiry, with full commitment to whatever Spirit deemed best. This process is essential for any developing intuitive.

Finding Your Service

Like many others, Sharon found her service by focusing on what she loves. Just as our guides use our imagination and frame of reference to communicate with us, Spirit likewise uses our outward personality and interests to help us spread light in the world. When we look to our passions and interests, we find a flow, a movement toward a way of life.

Our passions open us up emotionally, allowing us to be fully present and openhearted in our actions. If our passion is music, it's not just about the music itself but the act of creating it, the intention behind it, the hope for how this particular piece might reach people and bring them into their full presence, too. Whenever anyone becomes fully present, Spirit is happy. The whole universe celebrates our service.

So, what are you passionate about? What do you love doing? If the answer is readily accessible, follow it; if you need to automatic-write your answer or break out your oracle cards, do that. It may also be that you need to sit with this question for a while and let the answer unfold, or you may take this question to your Team in the practice presented near the end of this chapter.

Another way to connect with service is to look to our wounds. Grief, trauma, or anything else we've learned to either overcome or just simply live with is an excellent outlet for service. I once read for a woman who lost her daughter, and in her grief, she began to make phone calls to other women when they lost their children — women from her community and beyond, many of whom she had never met before. She would call them up and just listen, empathizing and making space for their heartbreak, only jumping in when necessary so they wouldn't feel alone. Sometimes she would go sit with them.

As the women who received these phone calls started to heal, some of them began to participate by also calling other women. They created a network offering support to bereaved mothers. I was so impressed by this initiative. To me, that is the ultimate service. Out of horrific grief, these mothers found a way to give of themselves — not only for their own healing but to genuinely help others in the same situation.

The network also provided grief education to help normalize the mothers' responses to profound loss. This is one of the most powerful forms of service: to teach what you yourself struggled the most to learn. I learned to trust my intuition and converse directly with my guides, and it changed my entire life — that is the driving force behind all the work I do as a teacher and mentor. Perhaps you've learned to get out of toxic relationships, so you set up a workshop to teach others to do that. Or maybe you have gained insight from a specific methodology, such as numerology or energy healing, and you want to explain what you've learned through a series of articles or videos. As connected as we are today, there are infinite opportunities to share what you know with others. Doing so takes whatever hardship you've faced and turns it into something constructive. It provides you with the option to transform your hard-won experience into an act of service.

I like to see this as an option, because it puts the focus on free will. Paying it forward is a choice. In this framework, it doesn't serve us to bypass the difficulty of what we've experienced; we're not brushing our painful emotions aside but gathering them toward us instead, concentrating them into a beam of light to point directly at what hurts. The woman who started the network of bereaved mothers is still grieving her daughter. She's not bypassing that at all. *With* that grief, not despite it or beyond it, she chooses to help someone else. This creates a kind of alchemy; her grief becomes something greater. Through that process, she can make meaning out of her experience.

This alchemical principle applies at all levels, right down to the smallest scale. It can be something as simple as lighting a candle at church for someone, even if they don't know about it. It can be a small, whispered prayer, a tiny moment of faith in the middle of profound emotional pain. Just the act of attempting to connect to someone else in the precise instant we feel most alone is transformative. In letting that impulse to serve others guide us, we allow the light into the darkest of places.

Each of these small acts of service means something. We never know what others are going through, really, and while they may not understand the totality of our experience, either, when we offer them service, we're offering them light. We're spiritual Lightworkers, after all. By nature, light spreads to the next person, and the next. That's just how it works. Service is simply our way of participating in that process.

Whether it's through passion or through wounding, it can help to start with small acts of service and just see what feels good. Sign up for a single volunteer shift, or go visit an elderly neighbor. If that feels too big, just start with saying a little prayer for someone else every day for a week. These tiny things start to open us to the alchemy of service — they begin to re-direct our energy into the flow of transformation. They build upon each other, creating an energy all their own.

The following practice will help you determine where your Team wants you to start.

PRACTICE

DIY Asking Your Guides

As we approach the end of this book, one of the biggest and most important gifts I can give you is permission to do it your own way. Your relationship with your guides is *yours*. I encourage you to communicate with your Team in your own voice; being 100 percent *you*, unedited. (If nothing else, consider that they probably know you and your flaws anyway — no need to adjust yourself, spruce things up, or hide in the shadows!)

Because things work best when they feel good, the practices you choose have to be aligned to your needs. At the beginning, it's important to go wide, exploring a variety of ways to make a connection. This approach can also serve you at other points along the way. When you feel stuck or uninspired, you can reach out for something new that calls to you. Yet all Lightworkers have their favorite go-tos. We each have an individual set of practices, tools, and methods that speaks most clearly to us.

This exercise offers two lessons. First, it does what it purports to do: help you connect with your guides to ask how you can be of service. Second, it provides an opportunity to explore doing things your own way.

This second lesson is profoundly important. Nowadays, there are thousands of guided meditations to choose from. There are millions of other books and exercises and workshops and teachers to lead you further down the path. And while those resources are awesome — I absolutely encourage you to get out there and explore them — the sheer abundance of what's available can detract from the honest truth, which is that *you're always going to receive the very best guidance from your own guides.* Always. And while part of *my* service is to tell you how to do that, part of my service is also to help set you free from the idea that you *need* to be told how to do it.

The premise of the practice is simple: ask your Team to show you your service. The rest is up to you. That means if you want to do this practice as a guided meditation, do it! Perhaps you'll want to use a Temple meditation like Creating a Psychic Contract presented in chapter 3, or adapt Meeting Hours in Heaven from chapter 4, asking for the guidance of a particularly wise loved one whose advice you trust. Maybe you'll want to write your meditation down, or dictate it slowly for yourself and play it back, or just envision it as you go. Maybe you'll do it on a mountaintop at a scheduled time, or maybe you'll sit down on the floor in the middle of your living room right now because you just *know* that this is your moment.

If you want to make it an automatic-writing session, fantastic! Get out your journal and a pen. You can write a guide's name at the top, or frame your question specifically, asking something like *How can I share my gifts? What form of service is best for me?*

Who needs me the most? What do I have to offer that I'm not see-ing? Where are there more opportunities to serve in my life? You can make a table with smaller, more specific questions, like *How can I serve in five minutes today? How can I start working toward greater service this week?*

You may be more called toward asking for a sign — or you may want to layer asking for a sign on top of your automatic writing or your meditation. Consider asking for a specific sign to show up when you're near someone you might serve or when you're over-looking an opportunity for service. Ask for another sign to show up whenever your service benefits someone else or to alert you to the joy that service brings *you.*

Then, to finish the exercise, translate it into action. Get out your phone or your calendar (or the calendar that's on your phone) and do something concrete: call or text the person you realized you might be specifically able to help right now, or schedule an action to take place in the next few days. If appropriate, get up and do something *right now.* Whenever we feel a call to serve and make even a small step toward enacting it, Spirit cheers, because we are aligning our free will with the guidance given to us.

Finally, the last step of the exercise is to acknowledge Spirit with gratitude. No matter how you chose to ask your Team about service, thank them for what you received. Bow down in gratitude for everything they have given you and continue to give you. I promise that if you do this, and if you continually work to act on the guidance you receive, they *will* keep the conversation going.

Service Feels Good

There's really only one way to know we're truly in service of the light, aligned with our Team's highest wishes for us: it just feels good. Perhaps the rest of our life feels good, and the ser-vice is the cherry on top. Or maybe the rest of our life feels absolutely awful, and what we're going through is so dark, but service provides a tiny ray of light. In both cases, the pleasure and joy of service capture our attention immediately. We *know* it is good because we can feel it.

That feeling has enormous power. It begins a ripple effect, pulling waves of light through us and blasting them out into the world. It's part of a greater movement toward light and wholeness — activating true self-worth, the final technique I will leave with you.

Chapter Ten

STAY POSITIVE AND KNOW YOU ARE WORTHY

Walking the Lightworker's Path

Throughout this book, I've hinted at the idea that psychic development often results in profound changes in self-worth. This realization came as a bit of a surprise for me. As I opened to spiritual lightwork, I watched with interest as the opinions and perceived opinions of others on certain topics quietly faded in importance — namely, I stopped caring what anyone thought or might think about me. I observed similar effects in the other students studying with me. And when I moved into the role of teacher and mentor, I witnessed this same phenomenon take place among the intuitives who came to me for help.

As I've explained, I believe that factors like strengthening boundaries, addressing fear, and developing a spiritual practice have a lot to do with this. This work encourages us to increase our reliance on Spirit's guidance, which naturally decreases our human tendency to look toward other people for suggestions or approval.

It's also because retrieving information from the psychic realm and delivering it to this plane requires us to directly confront self-doubt. Then we have to do it again … and again. Each time we face off with our doubt and choose confidence instead, we encode a new way of being.

Depending on how we approach it, this can be our superpower or our undoing. The number one thing I've seen holding people back in their psychic development is self-doubt. Sometimes the issue of self-doubt stays in the shadows and manifests as stalled or plateaued development. Other times, we're able to raise our concern through rhetorical questions: *Who am I to channel something beyond myself? Why would these powerful beings be choosing little ol' me to deliver their messages?* And, *What if I'm just on an ego trip here?*

These questions point to one of the greatest common misconceptions about psychic channeling: The idea that it's rare, or special, or somehow otherworldly. That it's meant for the chosen few, instead of the masses. That we have to be spiritually "good enough" to deserve it, but most of us simply aren't.

Ugh. I reject that line of thinking completely.

In fact, it rouses my own set of questions: *Why do you think you aren't worthy of channeling something beyond yourself? Why would these powerful beings* not *choose beautiful, powerful you to deliver their messages? Have you considered that it may be the ego telling you you're not worthy, because it's hammering in the idea that you and Source are somehow separate?*

The truth is that lots and lots of people can connect to

Spirit. Sure, there are degrees of ability, just like with anything else, but nearly everyone has at least some aptitude for psychic connection. Though this connection is extremely valuable, it isn't rare — it's common. Why wouldn't it be? Why would God just toss us out here, all alone? We're meant to receive divine guidance. We're supposed to connect in meaningful, heartfelt ways with our loved ones after they pass. It's just the ego, and all its ideas about separateness, that suggests otherwise. We are all worthy of receiving guidance from the light, each and every one of us. We don't have to be or do more to earn it, because we are already enough.

Understanding this shifts us into the realm of positivity, where our value is inherent and unshakable. It starts by changing the way we see ourselves. From there, this principle expands, shifting the way we see others as we awaken to their divine nature. This chapter explains more about that process, ending with my final vision: a world where people freely access the spiritual guidance waiting for them in the psychic realm. Staying positive and truly knowing our worth is the final technique I have to offer, because it's the culmination of everything I've written about until this point. It opens us to an entirely new paradigm: one that is eternal, infinite.

How Self-Worth Changes Us

Releasing our ego's need to make us small and separate shifts our understanding of our role in the divine plan. We learn that Spirit is within us and beyond us all at once. We begin to see that the light is in us and around us. This suggests that we are being supported — and then, as we receive confirmation through signs and messages, we have a direct experience of this support. We begin to trust.

Trust. In so many ways, trust is the beginning of everything.

It's what allows us to manifest. It's what gets us through the toughest times. It's an integral part of a joyful life.

Trusting life doesn't mean clinging to the false belief that everything will go our way. Instead, we trust the greater way — the highest intention and the highest path. We trust that whether something comes or it doesn't, it's ultimately the best result, because our guides are always looking out for what's in our interest in the long run. We trust that Spirit is seeing beyond the details and working toward the highest good of everyone involved.

At first, we just visit this state of trust, returning to doubt quickly afterward. Over time, we learn to sustain trust for longer periods of time. We start to understand that what comes to us is supposed to come to us and that we're perfectly entitled to say yes to it. We learn to trust so much in what we're being shown that it's preferable to just stay there. We don't want to go back to the darkness of doubt — we'd rather stay here, in the light.

This begins to release false ideas of cause and effect, many of which are just misunderstandings of how Spirit works. For instance, when our ego is overly involved in manifestation, it can mislead us, making us believe that we are the cause of our misfortunes. In some cases, we can even cloak this in spirituality, interpreting a challenge like a medical diagnosis, sudden layoff, or relationship dissolution as a "sign" that we've done something wrong. We've all seen terrible things happen to lovely people — as I mentioned in chapter 8, one of my good friends, Captain Sunshine, is currently healing from cancer. Though she most certainly sees her healing in a greater context, it doesn't involve self-blame. Her cancer isn't some sort of punishment or dark manifestation — instead, it's an opportunity to learn, heal, and love herself, all the while taking comfort in the knowledge that she's not alone and is worthy of her healing. She can find spiritual meaning in her cancer by accessing the guidance she needs to get through the moment. Notice that this, the most positive interpretation, is also the most helpful.

Living dedicated to the light doesn't ensure difficult things won't occur. Human life comes with all sorts of challenges. Instead, we can trust that everything difficult has the potential to teach us something, if we let it. I have no idea what Captain Sunshine's lesson is here, but it can't possibly be self-blame.

It's important to understand this, because it moves us away from thinking we have to fix what's out of our hands, instead shifting our goal to learning what we can from what arises. Suddenly, it's not *What did I do to deserve this difficult thing in my life?* but rather, *What does this have to teach me?* This allows us to respond without putting so much weight on the outcome. It demonstrates the trust we are building.

It also begins to release the habit of giving our power away to others. We stop over-apologizing and start owning who we are. This doesn't mean we should never apologize — sometimes, we mess up, and others deserve our honest acknowledgment of that — but rather that we don't need to apologize for the same thing over and over, and we certainly don't need to apologize for who we are. We also stop apologizing for our success. We learn to separate genuine humility, a divine value, from the search for approval, an ego-based addiction. We turn inward, looking to ourselves and our guides to indicate whether we're on the right path. When we misstep, we offer a genuine apology and move on, allowing ourselves to be fueled by self-forgiveness instead of waiting for forgiveness to arrive from an external source.

When we really step into a place of power and of seeking less to please others, our relationships can shift somewhat.

Some people may not be able to go there with us. If that feels uncomfortable, please know that it's temporary. Spirit always follows this up by bringing people of like mind — the type of people who don't want you to apologize for who you are but who want to celebrate your unique offerings to the world.

Transforming Relationships

Some people realize they need to make visible relationship shifts during this process. They may change their workplace, make changes to a romantic partnership, or grow closer to or drift further away from certain friends. This can be challenging, and it's trust that holds us, assuring us that some of the ones we have loved took us as far as they could and that the human connections that will best serve our new phase are on the way.

What's more common, however, is for most relationships to remain but start functioning differently. Our own upgraded self-worth translates into an increased sense of worth with others.

This starts with playing the devil's advocate to your own judgment. Thoughts like *She said that because she doesn't like me* begin to carry less weight. They're suddenly accompanied by follow-up thoughts like *Maybe she said that because she's having a bad day, and it has nothing to do with me at all.* Or *He shouldn't do that* becomes *I don't know why he's doing that, but perhaps he's being guided and there's a greater plan I don't fully understand.* Self-worth renders us genuinely humble in the face of judgment. We realize how much we *don't* know, and we back off, even if only within our own minds. This true humility doesn't make a dent in our self-worth. And, because we no longer seek the approval of others, we stop needing to approve of *them.* We realize that what someone else is doing is none of our business.

Now, here's where it gets really interesting, because releasing our own judgment has myriad benefits. One of the main ones is that we open ourselves to celebrate the success of others — regardless of whether it's reciprocated. What a breakthrough! This sometimes takes a little work, and this chapter's practice will help you get through it. It's a lesson I learned well — mostly because I had to.

You may remember elements of this story from chapter 1, when I introduced ego. Here, I'll give a little more detail, explaining how the story translates to self-worth. When I first started doing this work, my self-worth was less secure. I knew I was skilled, but I was also a total rookie, so I would get nervous around more outwardly successful psychics who had a larger following or who had been promoted by bigger names. I mistakenly conflated notoriety with worth — a common and entirely absurd assessment. This meant I always saw *their* success in relation to *my* success. Instead of relating — seeing everything we had in common — I separated, focusing on everything that was different and assigning those differences value. My competitive nature took over my thoughts. I just couldn't imagine, somehow, that we could both be successful; I couldn't see how Spirit was leading each of us down our own perfect path. Though I was generally kind and polite, I struggled somewhat to celebrate the gifts of others for fear that doing so would diminish my own by comparison.

The problem, of course, was the comparison. Once I got rid of that and started focusing on relatability instead, everything flowed. But I couldn't have done it without first understanding my own value.

Today, I'm connected with many other psychics. When I see someone else in my field reach a milestone, I celebrate, because they're showing me what's possible! I stand firmly in my own self-worth and just offer my support, reaching out to express my genuine joy with a small text or note that says, "I'm so happy for you. Thanks for representing us in such a beautiful way." It's a triumph over ego and judgment. This feels authentic because it is — I can honestly be proud of myself and proud of my peer at the same time. I can even *admire* them, experiencing true humility without decreasing my self-worth.

Perhaps this seems like only a tiny victory. After all, isn't this the type of friendship we've all been working on since we were coloring with crayons and building towers out of blocks? Yet actually feeling joy in the face of others' success is no small feat. It requires understanding that we do not possess *comparative* value but *inherent* value, and trusting that when everyone is doing their best work, we will all succeed together.

This happens between professional psychics, but it also happens with developing psychics in the classroom. Sometimes one student will download an entirely formed message, such as "Your grandfather Jim is here, and he's remembering that time he took you to the farm where he grew up. You said the sky was so blue, remember? No clouds. And he took you to the dairy barn, where they kept the cows, and through the cornstalk fields. That day was so special to him. He was so proud to share his childhood with his granddaughter...." Another student, meanwhile, is sitting there just blurting out freestanding words, like "Um... blue? Cheese. Bleu cheese?! No — just the color blue, and cheese. Corn?" It would be easy to judge one as a "better psychic" than the other. Indeed, many students do. But the truth is that these students are equally successful. They are each on their own journey, finding a way to connect with something beyond themselves. Their value does not come from comparison; it's bigger and truer than that.

Near the end of chapter 1, I asked you to keep an eye on

how you're naturally relating to seeing others succeed and to celebrate these successes whenever possible. I imagine that in some ways this was easy and in others it was more difficult — specifically, it was likely more difficult when there was a person or situation that brings up envy. Envy is based in the idea of comparison, and for most of us, comparison runs rampant throughout our daily interactions. Though we try our best, it affects many of our careers, friendships, and families. That's part of why this work is so transformative: when we let go of comparison, we can really start to focus on the soul and self. All this time and energy is freed up simply by dropping the habit of watching what somebody else is doing and judging ourselves.

Don't get me wrong — there's nothing wrong with healthy competition. The issue is when we put a value judgment on it, thinking (even subtly) that anyone is better or worse in the eyes of Spirit. This idea of better or worse is extremely damaging; it profoundly shifts the way we see people, and it's to our own detriment. That's because when we compare ourselves to others and let our envy tell us we aren't enough, we fail to recognize what Spirit is often trying to show us: our own potential.

That's right: there, on the flip side of envy, is our own desire. It's our ambition. It's our drive. We should absolutely exchange positive energy with the people we admire. They're showing us what's possible! They're demonstrating where we, too, can go. When our ego-based envy is in the way, we can't connect with them because we're blocking the flow. This is true for people we know personally and public figures. Transforming our envy into an affirmation of self-worth is therefore a highly valuable practice.

True self-worth blasts us out of other people's business and right into our own. People who understand this attract each other. My own journey out of comparison and into understanding the source of my value ultimately brought an amazing set of personal and professional friends into my life. My husband and kids are also incredible; their love makes this work possible. Today, I can clearly say that I'm better supported in the human realm than I could have ever dreamed of. Not only that, this support is just the cherry on top, because I'm sourcing most of what I need from the universe and myself. This allows me to enjoy the support of others all the more. Through finding a more positive way to interact with others, I've brought more positivity into my life.

From there, the possibilities get pretty exciting.

The Power of Positivity

What happens when a whole bunch of people awaken to the divine guidance available to them and truly feel supported? What is possible when we get out of the scarcity mindset, releasing comparison, and really start cheering for others? What is the collective result of our becoming Lightworkers, each of us tuning in to the frequency of the divine light while still walking on Earth?

One by one, we illuminate. From there, the light simply does what it's always done: it spreads.

Can you imagine the power of this? Can you contemplate thousands of people just spontaneously waking up to their own self-worth and wanting to remind others of *their* worth, too? Yes, getting psychic downloads is amazing. Reading for others, connecting them with their loved ones, is pretty cool as well. It's fun and fulfilling. But the potential of simply awakening people to the psychic guidance within so they can use it in their everyday lives seems so much greater to me. It's what called me to mentorship: the sheer potential and unmistakable power of positivity.

There are many ways to spread our positive energy and help others connect with Spirit. One is just to show up and be present, exactly as we are. Knowing we are worthy naturally invites others to do the same. It brings an energy, a sense of safety, that makes space for others to show up more authentically. Another option is to teach. That doesn't necessarily mean to teach intuitive development, as I do; it could mean teaching how you overcame whatever it is that you overcame to do this work. What allowed you to start channeling light? What did you have to face, release, develop, and so on? Helping others do the same *is* a form of spiritual lightwork, because it's paying it forward with gratitude to the source of that light. When we teach this, we're giving over what we learn and becoming the heart of the energy.

Still another way is to be open about our psychic connection without making it a bigger deal than it is. When we connect with our guides on a regular basis, it becomes extremely relaxed. There's no need to overthink it; we're just chatting with them. We're just checking in here and there. It's no different from how we talk to any other friend, except these ones don't have a physical body, and the conversation isn't necessarily happening out loud. And like any other friend, our Team can offer us tiny pieces of advice. We don't have to go to them with our big life questions every time; we can just check in and listen as they tell us to call so-and-so for a chat or to be kind to someone because they're having a hard time. Then we act accordingly.

As I've stated, it's not always necessary to share that the information is channeled. Sometimes this serves to make psychic connection seem more exotic, removed from this life. When we do share the origin, it helps to do so in a relaxed way, creating emotional safety around the idea. This makes it more emotionally safe for others to do the same. By normalizing psychic connection, we support everyone around us in living their very best lives. The energy exchange between people becomes positive and appreciative, and as a result, we create a happier world.

This is ultimately the best thing for all of us. Like our prayers, it's for the highest and greatest good of everyone involved.

Understanding this is one thing; putting it into action is another. As you progress, it's common to come up against blockages. The following exercise will help you through one of the main ones.

PRACTICE

··· ꓿)ꞏ⊙ꞏ(꓿ ···

Creating a Spiritual Mission Statement

One of the greatest blocks to receiving light is feeling difficult emotions like judgment and envy toward others.

Both come from comparison. When we compare and we come out on top, we feel judgment: *Why isn't she handling that better? I would.* Or *I'm sure that if it were up to me, I would have done things more effectively.* When we compare and lose, in our own estimation, we feel envy: *Why is he enjoying that success?* Or *Really, that should be me; I deserve what they have.*

This habit is entirely human, and it's intimately tied to self-worth. It nearly always comes from scarcity thinking — that there is only one "right" way to be, that there is not enough success / good fortune / happiness for everyone — and it nearly always feels terrible when we fall victim to it. Sure, we can get lost in our own internal rant, but in the end there's at least some part of us that is aware we're feeling this way about others. These sorts of nagging thoughts about other people's business are uncomfortable and draining.

Plus, this thinking reinforces one of the massive fears that accompanies low self-worth: that we ourselves will be condemned, just as we are condemning others.

Seriously, how can we move forward like *that*?! All that energy is nasty and negative. The purpose of this exercise is to help you shake off these negative emotions, transforming them into helpful factors that can further your path. We don't need to bypass them, but we don't need to dwell on them, either; instead, we can address them and move on.

There's something else to be gained by working through these emotions. This process can be instructive if we direct our attention toward what our negative emotions are trying to show us. Usually, buried within our most firmly held grievances are clues to what matters the most to us. Within frustration we can find hints about what we came here to do — our spiritual mission. We just have to dig a little bit to get at them.

Ready? For part I of this exercise, you'll need a journal and a pen. If necessary, ground yourself. Take some deep breaths and cue your guides that you're ready to get to work.

Part I

Start by listing the ways you judge yourself and others. Catalog your grievances about the world. What bothers you? What do you wish people would understand or be better at? What do you wish you could see, experience, or have? What feels unfair? Tell the truth! Be brutally honest, as this is just for you; you'll burn the paper when you're done, if you like!

When your thoughts feel complete, take a moment to collect yourself. Allow the emotion to be there without making it right or wrong.

Then look down at your paper. Read back what you wrote,

searching for clues that might indicate what matters most to you. For instance, if you're angry because you judge someone to be acting selfishly, perhaps this indicates that selfless service is important to you. If you're envious of the breadth of someone else's influence, this may come from an honest longing to express yourself on a public platform. Look for the positive interpretations and write them down as they arise.

If your negative emotions are aimed at someone specific, circle or underline any words that connect you to the other person. Where can you relate? For instance, if the person is really talented at something you're working to develop, can you see that you're both seriously dedicated to the same pursuit? If the person is doing something you deem to be "wrong," can you see how they're searching for something you value, too? Can you empathize with the factors that may have gone into their choice? What do you admire in this person, and how can you cultivate those qualities?

Now, look at the notes you've taken and the words you've underlined. How is Spirit showing you the areas in which you can grow? What are your emotions showing you about your self-worth, your purpose, your spiritual mission?

If this was a lot, cleanse and ground yourself. Finish the practice for today and resume with part II another day. You may also begin part II now, if you're ready.

Part II

It's time to translate the work you did in part I into your spiritual mission statement. This is your *goal*: the way you are meant to spread light in the world. (At least, for now! You can always go back and update it later, as you're guided.) It's important to note that while your spiritual mission is likely deeply tied to your service, they aren't exactly the same thing. While your service usually involves a *what* and often includes a *who*, your mission is much more specific, because it also includes *why* you do your service.

For this part of the exercise you'll once again need your journal and a pen. You may also want a sheet of loose-leaf paper.

Just like with psychic interpretation, there's always a positive way to interpret what the world is giving us. Ask yourself what the most positive way to translate the emotions, grievances, and longings you uncovered in part I would be. How could you process these factors so they not only get out of your way but also help you move forward?

On a clean sheet of paper — perhaps even a fancy one, but any simple notebook paper ripped from a journal will also do — write your name and the words *Spiritual Mission Statement*.

Then take a few minutes for yourself. Connect with your guides. This is a DIY process, so do whatever you need to do to bring all your presence and support into this moment.

When you're ready, ask your guides: "What is my spiritual mission?" Remember to think in terms of *what*, *who*, and *why*.

Example 1: Luke

Luke is a healer and bodyworker. He loves his job, but he sometimes finds himself judging his clients and friends for the way they care for their bodies, such as when they return to a poor diet after a cleanse or forgo exercise. He also gets particularly upset when he sees news reports about local environmental contaminants, blaming politicians for not doing a better job of protecting their constituents. In part I of this exercise, he realized he strongly values well-being as a right and wants to promote that not only through his healing work but also through local environmental activism.

Luke's Spiritual Mission Statement

"My mission is to promote well-being through healing with my hands and working to create a healthier environment through local activism."

Example 2: Kendal

Kendal is a stay-at-home mom. While she loves being at home with her kids, she often loses her cool when they fight with each other — which seems like all the time lately! But when she's able to stay calm, the guidance on communication she receives from her Team helps her kids a lot. She also notes that she gets triggered by small dramas in her extended family or circle of friends — even if she's not involved herself — and dwells on them. Kendal longs to make some sort of income while she's at home and frequently tunes in to livestreams and podcasts hosted by other moms, but she also feels jealous of them, like she wants the same success. In part I of this exercise, Kendal saw that peaceful communication is truly important to her and found that she wants to share that both in her personal life and with the world.

Kendal's Spiritual Mission Statement

"My mission is to create a part-time online business teaching the communication techniques my guides have shared with me and promote them to other moms, with the goal of spreading peace in the world."

Example 3: Lisanne

Lisanne loves to sing. When other people are slightly out of tune, though, or when the drumbeat is off, she wants to scream. She has found a strong connection to channeling through automatic writing. Often she hears a tune while she writes, as if there were a melody to go along with her words. In part I of this exercise, Lisanne connected with her desire to help other musicians understand that music is just a divine download.

Lisanne's Spiritual Mission Statement

"My mission is to host a series of workshops for musicians, helping them connect with their guides so that the divine sound flows through the world more freely."

As you can see, spiritual mission statements can vary a lot. They don't need to be long-term, either; they can shift as our guidance shifts.

To close, I want to add a final example.

Example 4: MaryAnn

MaryAnn is a professional psychic medium whose soul is fed by her daily, ongoing connection with Spirit. When talking about this with others, she was often disappointed by how those not in the psychic world framed psychic connection as something exotic, otherworldly, or hard to reach. MaryAnn realized that she placed a high value on the empowerment that comes with opening to Spirit, and that she wanted everyone to have a direct experience of their divine guidance.

MaryAnn's Spiritual Mission Statement

"My mission is to strengthen intuition in others via developing a public platform to mentor other intuitives, helping them feel guided and supported throughout their daily lives and awakening them to their unique spiritual mission."

When you've finished, you can decorate your mission statement or leave it as is. You can post it on your bedroom wall — or, if you're called, on the internet. You can recite it every morning for ten days straight or secretly tell your very best friend or stash it in your keepsake box. This is your mission, your process! The only thing I ask is that you *take your mission statement seriously.* Now that you've written it down, you're accountable for making your mission happen, on whatever scale works for you!

That starts with believing you are worthy of it. *You're worthy of your spiritual mission!* There is nothing you need to do, be, or accomplish to become worthy of it, because your guides designed this mission precisely for you — in fact, that's what they've been trying to show you all along. Believe it. Let yourself feel your inherent worth.

Finally, we'll close this practice with gratitude. Don't forget to thank your guides — and yourself — for bringing you this far. Really sit with gratitude for a couple of minutes to finish the exercise.

An Infinite Exchange with the Universe

The truth is that those simple things like joy, light, and love can move mountains.

The reason for this is that connecting with positivity raises our vibration. We summon the light, and by doing so, we connect with others doing the same. This amplifies the positivity on the planet.

We have every reason to participate in this exchange. How convenient that the very thing we can do to help the world is also the thing that helps *us*! It feels more powerful than anything we've known. When we enter into this flow, we no longer doubt. Genuine self-worth skyrockets, while the ego takes a back seat. Our relationship with Spirit becomes, simply, everything.

It's an amazing moment when we reach this threshold. We suddenly feel the security of knowing we are divinely protected and always will be. We are reminded, every second of every day, that we are not alone. Our guides *always* have our back. They're watching, responding, and communicating with us — all we have to do is awaken to what has been true for eternity.

Raising our vibration also amplifies positivity in other realms. By consciously calling their divine energy here and working to send our light back to them, we create a consistent flow, an exchange of energy that is celebrated both here on Earth and on the higher psychic planes. Our Team is here to support us, and they want to do their job! When we let them, we extend the very best of ourselves back to the light in gratitude. It's always well received.

When I envision this flow of light between us and the universe, I see an illuminated infinity symbol. I see a never-ending river of energy flowing between this frequency and another. It's a beautiful reminder that our connection to the universe, to God, is infinite. It goes on and on and on. I find that really comforting, because I know we are a part of Spirit and Spirit is a part of us. We're interdependent. We need each other.

We are part of the story line of this beautiful universe.

The moment we really, truly recognize that, we enter into alignment with everything. We become infinite.

ACKNOWLEDGMENTS

"It's time to write another book!" said my guides. Without hesitation, I answered, "Let's do it!"

This book and its words have been requested by many, including my guides! But this book could not have been possible without the divine guidance and support from the following people. My gratitude for you all is limitless.

To my beautiful soul sister Gabrielle Bernstein: Gabby, your friendship and support through these past years have been a precious gift to my life. I am forever grateful that Spirit led us to each other. I love you.

To Chandika: Thank you for hearing my voice along with the voice of Spirit and artfully displaying them within the pages of this book. It's because of your beautiful talents that we have these words to share with the world.

To my literary agent Michele Martin: You stuck with me and this project through a time that made your job incredibly difficult. Thank you! Thank you for pushing me to do better and more. Thank you for challenging me. Most of all, thank you for believing in me and this book. I appreciate all that you have done for me.

To my editor Georgia Hughes and the team at New World Library: You saw the numbers and you said yes anyway! You said yes because you believe in the integrity of the "work," and I am the grateful recipient of that integrity. Your attention to detail and to supporting the light-filled intention of this book has been stellar.

To my team: Jane and Stephen, thank you for being a force of knowledge and support. You both have believed in me and this work, and I am forever grateful for your time and your patience. Your guidance has been transformative in so many ways. You are two of the most generous people I have ever met. I love you both. The sky's the limit! Thank you to the mysterious Sue. There is a reason our clients love to talk to you. Your warm heart and gentle patience are felt by all. Thank you for being with me through this crazy journey for as long as you have. I love you, my beautiful friend. To Jaspre, Spirit put us in each other's paths, and I am forever grateful. I am looking forward to doing more beautiful work with you. You are a Lightworker!

To my students and fellow budding Lightworkers: When you learn, you teach. It has been my honor to open you up to all that Spirit can bring to your life and to the lives of others. You all have inspired me to write this book and share more of what I continue to learn. My wish for you is that you go and spread the light!

To my beautiful NoFo friends who have been with me for years: You have seen my life move through many chapters. You have stood by me with love, free of judgment and with full support. I thank you. I appreciate you. You are all a forever part of my heart.

To Dorene, Diana, Nikole, Christine, and Teresa: 11:11, 1:11,

2:22, 3:33, 4:44, 5:55, and 10:10 because it's a thing! Thank you for being the beautiful souls that you all are. You have each given me love and laughter throughout the years, and I am blessed to call you friends.

To Kristina Grish: Thank you for sharing your talents early on in this project. Your love and support are a valued treasure in my life. As are you.

To Pat Longo: So much of my work now stems from the beautiful foundation that you so graciously set up for me. You will always be part of my spiritual story. For that, I am proud and grateful.

To my husband Chris: You have been and are my forever friend. Thank you for all you do for our family. You are tireless when it comes to supporting us and loving us. Thank you for honoring my wings and encouraging me to fly. Our souls know our story, and what a story it is! It's been quite a journey. I love you.

To my beautiful children: You are the most precious parts of my heart and my soul. I feel blessed to be your mom. Your support means the world to me. I love you. I hope you always hear the guidance and flow with it.

To my sweet furry baby Phoenix: Your handsome face and kind demeanor put a smile on so many faces. Thank you for giving me the healing breaks my mind needs. You are pure joy.

To my family: Thank you to my parents and siblings for all the love, support, and honesty you have given me throughout the years. I love you all so very much. I am grateful and honored to be your daughter and sister.

And finally, thank you to Spirit, God, Source, guides, angels, and my loved ones on the Other Side. Leaning into the light and trusting the journey I've been asked to go on has been life changing. I am blessed. I am grateful. Thank you for giving me the words to serve.

ABOUT THE AUTHOR

Maryann DiMarco, the "Medium Mentor," is an internationally recognized psychic medium, author, healer, and spiritual teacher. After learning to meditate at the age of five, she began consciously developing her connection with Spirit in adulthood. Today, she offers validating and positive one-on-one sessions, powerful group readings, individual mentorship for mediums and the like, and workshops for developing psychics.

MaryAnn has been a featured expert across various media platforms, including the *New York Times*, *The Dr. Oz Show*, *Women's Health*, *Elle*, and *Redbook*, and a speaker at Gabrielle Bernstein's Masterclass. Her first book, *Believe, Ask, Act: Divine Steps to Raise Your Intuition, Create Change, and Discover Happiness*, was released in 2016. She lives on the North Fork of Long Island with her husband and two children.

For more, please visit www.MaryAnnDiMarco.com.